LIFE START *to* FINISH

THIS BOOK ANSWERS THE IMPORTANT QUESTIONS

Robert Todd

BALBOA. PRESS
A DIVISION OF HAY HOUSE

Balboa Press books may be ordered through booksellers or by contacting:

Balboa Press
A Division of Hay House
1663 Liberty Drive
Bloomington, IN 47403
www.balboapress.com.au
1 (877) 407-4847

Print information available on the last page.

ISBN: 978-1-5043-0223-4 (sc)
ISBN: 978-1-5043-0224-1 (e)

Balboa Press rev. date: 08/12/2016

Thank you to those who helped me put this book together.

I dedicate this book to my wife Judy
who throughout my life
supported, helped, and guided me
to achieve the knowledge I have now.

CONTENTS

PART 1

PART 2

PART 3

Part 1

MANY QUESTIONS

As a management consultant and trainer in the area of interpersonal skills and verbal communications for 23 years and 20 years as a counsellor and clinical hypnotherapist, I have been asked many times if I would write a book. At other times I was told to write a book. One of the strangest was when I was attending one of those Mind Body and Soul conferences which I rarely attend, sometimes out of curiosity. I was standing right at the back, almost hidden from the person who was presenting on stage. She said "That gentleman in the back wearing a leather jacket." I looked around to see who it was and it was actually me. She said "You have to write a book" I replied, "you're kidding" and walked away. I keep getting requests to write this book and answer some of the questions I had been asked in training and counselling sessions.

Questions such as:

What is life all about?
Why do I seem to have so many problems at this time?
Why are there some things I wish for come true and other times I get the opposite?
Why it is children in the same family can be so different from each other?

Why did I pick this particular partner?
Why do I have certain habits or phobias?
Why do I have likes and dislikes that seem to make me different from others?
Does the environment have an effect on or make me?
Does what has happened in the past, have to rule my future?
Why am I here?
What am I here to learn?
Do I just have to learn to cope?
Is there any purpose to this earth?
Is there a God?
What happens when I die?
Is there an afterlife?

There are many questions to which people want to know the answer, sometimes out of curiosity and other times necessity. I'm sure you can think of some more.

Throughout this book I hope I can answer your questions and give you insights into how you can make your life more enjoyable, more effective, achieve your goals, and help you to understand what is really happening.

I will give you many examples of other people's experiences. I hope you will see there are ideas and examples that you can associated to your problems, thereby providing you with new ideas and ways to solve your problems or answer your questions.

The past is the past, it is over and done. We can't change the past. On the other hand we can certainly change the future. I believe that if we continue to get a problem over and over, obviously we are not responding or are seeking alternative solutions to the problem. In some cases we believe the situation is normal and in extreme cases some people even believe harmful relationships are acceptable.

Come with me on a journey of discovery, a journey that took me many years. As you read my and other peoples experiences, it will give you insight into what's going on in your life; then maybe you too will have a journey of discovery.

The first part of the book covers how I discovered the answers to these questions. The second part of the book headed The New Adventure is a series of case studies to explain where the information in the book was developed and the third part Life Start to Finish puts it all together giving you all the information about life before you were born, why your parents acted as they did, what made you think as you do, then right through to death and after. Often the world we live in is different from what we perceive.

INTRODUCTION

What are your beliefs?

I know through experience, my beliefs have changed. Over many years the experiences you have had, brought you to the conclusions that govern much of your life and attitudes. I know in some cases I have made dramatic changes to my belief system, because of the events that have taken place. This is an attempt to share my opinions and how they came about.

If there is anything within this book that causes you to rethink, then my book has been successful. I state clearly this is only my opinion from my experiences and I hope it gives you some points to think about in your life.

I was raised a Methodist, now called the Uniting Church. At a very young age I accepted what I was taught. It seemed to make great sense, although as I progressed some of the logic I developed certainly seemed to challenge the theories, for example, one belief was, when you die your body goes into the earth and at the time of the resurrection everyone will rise up and rejoice.

It is claimed; there have been six billion people previously born on earth and we now have seven billion living at this time. If the earth was to end today as some claim and all the past people were resurrected then there would be thirteen billion people and if the earth does not come to an end for many years how many souls would there be to fit on this planet? This no longer seems logical because these days I know the body would rot away and return to the earth. We also say ashes to ashes and dust to dust and I guess that is also applicable for cremation, where many ashes are scattered to the wind. Then we were told, when you go to heaven, you will live forever with God. How long is for ever, eternity, infinity?

I recently saw a program on TV where it was claimed the Earth would last for another three billion years. That's a long time to live in heaven after having only had a short time on earth, supposedly three score years and ten which obviously is not true, because some children die very early, some at birth, others live to the ripe old age of over one hundred.

My belief in God, heaven, eternity and spending the rest of my days there no longer seemed feasible. In fact it scared me, because I can remember some of the church people saying "He's gone to do what he liked most, play cricket all day, in heaven with his friends or maybe sing in the choir." Oh boy! I could not imagine myself in a situation for the next three hundred billion years or eternity, playing cricket or singing in a choir or even playing baseball as in the movie *Field of Dreams.*

Now let's look at other possibilities. Let's look at the logic if there is any, behind these views. What if there is no God or heaven and all this is a fallacy?

If someone believes there is nothing after this life and they die. If there is nothing, then at that point they will not know what they have believed is true. For there will be nothing. If someone believes there is a God and they die and there is nothing then they also will not know they were wrong as there will be nothing.

If they believe there is nothing and there is something when they die, they may suddenly realise that there is something and they will not believe they are dead, because they will not know exactly what is going on. If they believe there is a God and heaven, when they die they will realise they have changed dimensions and it will not be such a shock. I guess they will have proved they were right.

Therefore the question is, are you better to believe there is something? Because then, it will not be such a shock if there is!

There is a story about heaven. This guy dies and goes to heaven and he's incredibly impressed with what he sees. He walks around heaven looking at all the different sites and sounds. He is so happy and amazed. Then he comes to this area where there is a large brick wall and a sign that reads "Do not go within one hundred meters of this wall." He doesn't quite understand why it would be a restricted area or why the wall was even there. He goes to a previously departed family member who had been there for some time and asked them. "What's behind the brick wall?" the family member answers. "If you are quiet I'll show you." They creep over to the wall and listen. He can hear voices on the other side. He goes to talk and is told to keep quiet. They walk back a hundred meters from the restricted zone and when they get there he asked the question "What's on the other side?" And the answer surprises him. "That's a different religious group; they don't believe we make it here."

Some people say they could see other people in the room just prior to their death relatives and friends that had passed over. Some people who have had near-death experiences, claim they hover over the body and realise it is a choice as to whether they live or die.

If there are family members meeting you, or other things taking place such as the light the tunnel and guides, then you will understand and be familiar with the concept. It will not be unexpected.

I realised I was better off thinking there was something there. I accepted it with what people call Faith, the ability to accept something without proof. This did not really satisfy me and I guess I kept asking the question. What is reality? Is there a God, a Universal Mind? A place we go as spirits other than this Earth?

Not having made a definitive decision, I left the question very open and this is what took me on the adventure of my life. It enabled me to form opinions totally different from what I had been taught, totally different to what other people perceived I could only go on what I observed and this has formed my opinion which I now offer to you for your consideration.

Let's me start to answer your questions.

THE JOURNEY BEGINS

I have conducted and attended many courses in my lifetime. There was one course in which we were told we should program for parking spots. This was something new to me and as I tend to learn by observation. I decided I would give it a go. That night I was going to a restaurant for dinner. We had been told to see ourselves driving into the exact parking spot we required. To my surprise, it worked. Being the open-minded sceptic that I am, I thought it probably was just a fluke.

The next day the instructor asked us how our exercise had turned out. Some of the participants said they had success, some said they had tried and it sort of worked and others hadn't tried it at all. I thought it was interesting that some people had not even tried.

The following day we were introduced to our guides during a meditation. Once again I found this exercise interesting. I received a male Guide named Monomer and female Guide named Ann.

I went home and described Monomer to my wife Judy. He was old, slightly hunched, hard of hearing and wearing old casual clothes from about the Roman era. My female Guide Ann was dressed in a green suit, was up to date and very precise in every detail, including the fact that every hair on her head had obviously been placed in the correct position. Judy started to laugh. I asked, "What was funny?" She replied "This is symbolic of your two personalities. At home you dress in old clothes, you don't listen to the children as much as you should, this is why Monomer is partly deaf, yet at work you're like Ann precise and accurate and even when you set out your course material the pencils and rubbers must be in an exact place."

I suddenly realised that my guides were symbols of my lifestyle.

I decided to experiment, I placed a handkerchief on a pencil and cleaned out Monomer's ears. To my surprise, Judy mentioned about a week later that I was now listening more to the children and her.

Question: Was it the comment Judy made about me not listening, or the fact that I had cleaned Monomers ears that made the difference? In other words, were the symbols of my guides just my mind giving me a message and were not really spirit guides, as we had been told? I had to find out.

Do we have spirit guides?
Are they real or are they imagination?

The answer to this question came very quickly. I was telling some friends about the imaginary guides. They suggested I visit a woman on the audio counter at David Jones (a major retail store); she is a very good clairvoyant. Off I went to David Jones and located this person. As soon as I met her, I asked if she was a clairvoyant. She said; "There are two people standing one above your left shoulder and one above your right shoulder." and she went on to describe my spirit guides in full detail. Obviously these guides are real. She also mentioned that above me was a large painting with an ornate gold frame. She said it was an old master. I was rather taken aback and I'm not sure if she meant it was a painting of an old master or it was an old master painting.

IMPORTANT POINT 1: I now had confirmation my Guides were real.

After experiencing success many times with parking I included the concept into my management courses. I also found some people did it with success, some said they tried it while others never gave it a chance. I soon realised there were three groups of people. The first group believed it would work and were successful, the second group thought it might work and sometimes it did. The third group were not game to try, in case it worked, because if it did then they would have to accept the world was different than what they believed. It would challenge their belief system and this would mean many of the decisions they had made in the past could have been wrong.

Question: I wonder which group you fall into.

Are you willing to change your belief system?
Do you accept new ideas?
Are you going to give it a try?

Are you so programmed into your current beliefs, that to change any of them would create tension and you rationalise the situation to maintain stability?

I believe this book will challenge many of your beliefs as the experiences I had challenged mine. There were many times that made me rethink my concepts.

For example, on one occasion in one of my courses I was talking about parking spots. At lunchtime, one of the guys in the course challenged me to prove it. We drove towards the restaurant and I said "We will drive into a parking spot at the back of the hotel," when we arrived there was no parking spot. I said "We need to wait about 30 seconds" he laughed and said there's a spot further up. My

Guide reminded me and I said "No, that is too small we will drive into the parking space allotted for us." Again he laughed and drove forward to the spot further up, which was too small for him to get into easily. He persisted and after backing and forwarding a number of times he finally parked, only to look back at where my guide had told me there was a parking spot coming, to see that three cars had pulled out and we would have driven in if we had waited. I asked my guide "What went wrong?" The answer I got was:

IMPORTANT POINT 2: "You can't prove this to anyone they just have to have the faith to do it."

This was a big lesson for me, a lesson that changed my belief system and I remembered it said in the Bible, "Test not your God."

I had started talking to my guides regularly. It seemed if I asked a question the answer would come very quickly into my mind. In many cases, they were not what I expected.

Even the name of my guides fascinated me. Most people had names that were standard such as John or Peter and my female Guide Ann. I looked up the meaning; it meant grace, mercy, or prayer.

So what about my male guide named Monomer? This was rather a strange name, which I did not understand. I had no idea why I would receive such a strange name. Each course I conducted, I asked everyone if they knew what Monomer stood for.

It wasn't long before someone told me that it was actually a chemical term meaning, a basic building block or starting point. So even the name of my Guide had a symbol contained within it. I guessed it was the start to a new area of learning.

YOUR GUIDES

Let's talk about your guides, they are real. They have been with you for a long time. They are not there to make decisions. That would take away your Free Will. They are there to help you achieve your goals and help you learn by experience.

It's interesting to note, your guides do things for you, even if you do not know they exist. You do not have to talk to them or give them thanks.

Remember when I first met my male guide. I told you he was partly deaf and Judy said that represented me. My guide was not deaf, he was just giving me a message about myself.

IMPORTANT POINT 3: Guides talk telepathically.

This is a very important point to remember, because when you communicate, which you are doing many times in the day, as far as your guides are concerned what you visualise is what you desire.

IMPORTANT POINT 4: You get what you concentrate on.

If I say "don't think of an orange," you have to first think of an orange to understand what I said. Therefore if you express the words "I don't want" then you visualise what you don't want. Your guides only receive the visual image, and think that is what you do want.

IMPORTANT POINT 5: Your guides carry out their activities with unconditional love, no judgement and as you requested.

This also applies when you make a judgement; you see something you don't like and you visualise it. Even though you are opposed to it, the Guide sees the image and draws what you don't want to you.

Guides will not give you lotto numbers; they can only confirm the numbers you pick are what you want. They will not make decisions for you. They are there to Guide you not take away your free will.

If someone judges people with money negatively and they see themselves short of money, their guides will manifest just that and the person will never have enough money. This is what keeps people poor. What a person believes is what they get. Look at Lotto winners after three years; fifty percent are broke and according to statistics after seven years, only three precent have any wealth left. Some people even say it was the worst thing that happened to them.

IMPORTANT POINT 6: Whatever you fear or love you create. Whatever you judge you create and whatever you question you create.

Your guides bring the answer to you sometimes in dramatic ways. Be aware if you visualise something and say or think how could someone do that? Your guide will bring it to you, to answer your question. Be careful what you ask for.

If someone has a problem with anger, jealously, impatience, or other negative feeling and they ask their guide to help remove these situations from their life. Their guide cannot stop them having negative feelings. Guides can't interfere with free will. The person will probably ask by saying "I don't like this situations" and visualise it as it is. Then say "I will stay calm and relaxed." Their guide will receive two images and thinks this is what the person wants. The guide then brings more negative situations, into the person's life. By doing this, the person will have more opportunities to learn by experience. Their guide may also bring people who can teach them different techniques to handle their emotions.

Sometimes when you set a new goal and have it clear in your mind, you may get events from the past reoccurring. These may be contrary to your new goals. The reason is your guide has gone through your past experiences and noticed there are times when you had contrary opinions. The guides bring the situation back into your life so you can either confirm or change your previous attitude. They are asking you, "Is this what you want or your new goal?" This may happen several times and each time it occurs it is important for you to reinforce your new goal.

Your Life line and previous decisions you need to change.

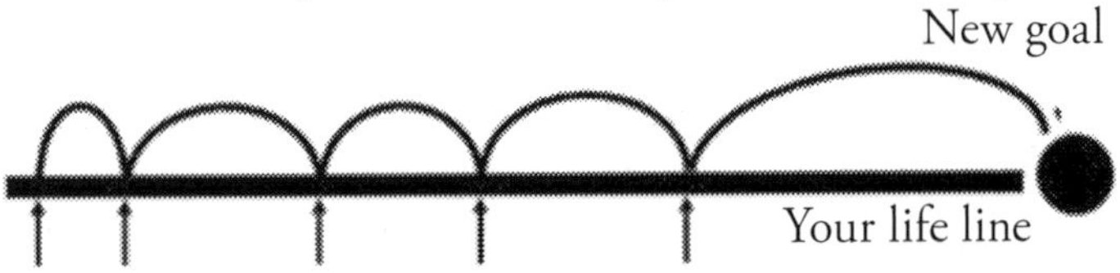

YOUR GUIDES CREATE SITUATIONS TO CONFIRM OR CHANGE PREVIOUS BELIEFS

Throughout your life as you develop, your guides may change in appearance and age. My first guide, Monomer, was old, deaf and Jewish. He eventually turned into a 26 year old well-dressed male. As I changed, Ann also changed from the precise green suit with every hair in place to where she was wearing more relaxed clothes.

Many years later Quintrex became my new guide and she was wearing a white top and long yellow patio dress.

One night, two new guides suddenly appeared above the end of my bed. I must have asked the question about how we receive things in the physical world. One of the guides was behind a desk, I asked his name. He said it was "Simon." I asked what he did. He said it was his job to bring into my life the physical things I requested. I then asked "Why his name was Simon, as most of my guides had different or very meaningful names?" He said this was no different, because his name was simple and that's exactly how the physical world is, simple.

IMPORTANT POINT 7: "You ask, we arrange, you receive."

"What about health?" I asked

IMPORTANT POINT 8: "Health is different", He replied. "It is a symbol of your thinking."

Then I remembered a book Judy often referred to on health by Louise L Hay "Heal Your Body" which explains all the symbols.

I asked the guide standing beside him who he was. He replied "I am the apprentice; they call me The Boy." I said, "Out of respect I could not call you The Boy. I will call you Big Boy," I asked him what he did; he replied "I study the psychology of what happens when Simon brings the things you request into your life."

The next week, Judy and I went to a psychic fair. Someone showed my wife a number of cards that were face down, naming all the Ascended Masters, they asked her to select one. When she turned it over it was the card for the Ascended Master Metatron; this meant nothing to us.

Later that day, a second person offered Judy to select any card from a pile of cards. Once again, she selected a card turned it over and again it was the Master Metatron. We thought it was strange at the time and must have some sort of message. When we went home, Jude looked up a book on the ascended masters. It said Metatron was known as "The Boy." That made us take notice. Often when we have something happen, we think is a coincidence or just luck. This is far from the truth; everything that happens in life has a purpose.

A few years ago, another guide suddenly appeared; his name was Abdulla, and again I was not sure what Abdulla meant. I asked him what he did and why he was there. He told me he was my protection. Now Abdulla was approximately 8 foot 6 inches tall and had a blue tinge to his skin. His arms were folded in front of him. I asked "What do you do?" "Do you threaten people to keep them from harming me?" He said "No I just talk to their guides, send them love and tell them they have nothing to fear from you and you are only here to help." I asked him how long he had been protecting me. He told me for a long time. I said "You must be disappointed because I did not know you existed till now and I have never thanked you for protecting me." His reply surprised me "I do not work for you." I said "That is strange as you are my protector. "Who do you work for?"

He said,

IMPORTANT POINT 9: "I work for God and as long as he is happy, that's all that counts."

As I went around I asked people if they knew what the name Abdulla meant. After a while, someone told me that it meant servant of God.

IMPORTANT POINT 10: Therefore, if he works for God, God must exist.

Many strange things can happen when you pay attention and listen carefully to your guides. They are there to help. They provide unconditional love, no judgement and as you request, whether it's good or bad for you. Some people do not have goals so their guide cannot manifest something that does not exist.

Others people are always trying to prove they are hard done by and their guide will even help them to do this by manifesting hard times. If you visualise things you fear, your guide will help you by creating situations to bring fear into your life. Whatever you fear, you create. In this way you learn to overcome your fears. Whatever you judge you create, so you learn not to judge. Whatever you question, you create and any questions you ask, are always answered sometimes, not as you expected.

By now I was meditating every day. I was quickly learning the correct way to talk my guide's language.

IMPORTANT POINT 11: Listen very carefully to your guides, for they only talk in positive terms.

I realised I must do the same. Your guides will bring the positive goal towards you. You must always say and visualise what you do want.

IMPORTANT POINT 12: They will pick up the visual of what you do want and bring it to you.

Remember, they communicate telepathically.

I started to teach this attitude in my courses and one example comes to mind. A company in Victoria started a so-called safety program where they had a sign with a red circle and a line through it and the words NO ACCIDENTS printed across the centre line. I suggested to the people at the course they should not use this sign. They should in fact use a triangular sign which was yellow with the words printed THINK SAFETY.

Three months later, I returned to the same company and their accident rate had reduced by 3%. They informed me, the accident rate of people who had used the original sign with the NO ACCIDENTS actually increased. I wondered what the company was doing about this and asked my guide if he could let me know. On the flight home on the company plane, I received the answer. I sat next to one of the senior executives. He told me they were in a dilemma. They had spent 3 million on a safety program and the only group that had not increased were the ones who refused to use the NO ACCIDENTS signage. All other groups had increased by 7%. The dilemma was, should we close the program or try to make it work? It is interesting to note one sign includes a negative word, accidents (fear), and the other a positive word, safety (love)

The next time I went to the same company I said I had run a course in New Zealand and a manager had a book called *Arigo Surgeon of the Rusty Knife*. I said I would like to have a copy; I believed it was only sold in New Zealand. As we were talking about programming the group challenged me to get the book, without buying it and they would know what I said was true. I said "yes" and turned it over to the universe.

IMPORTANT POINT 13: I had learnt not to try and prove anything; I also trusted the universe knowing it fulfils any request in the most appropriate way for our learning and at the perfect time.

We went on with the course and I didn't think of it again.

Three months later I returned; there were twelve new people in this group. They started to introduced themselves, the first three people were managers and the third person said "You said you would get the book Arigo Surgeon of the Rusty Knife and we would know if you got it for free." They must have asked the previous group about the course and were told of the request. Suddenly one of the participants stood up and said "Is that all you want, my mother gives me heaps of those silly books, I have one at home you can have it, I don't even know why I'm in the course. Everyone here are managers and I'm just a worker." He left the room, came back in half an hour with the book and dropped it on my desk and left. We didn't see him again. So what happened fulfilled the request; I got the book for free and they witnessed it without me doing a thing. Was it coincidence? No, things like this were happening to me on many occasions. The more positive I became, the clearer my images were with full trust in my guides.

IMPORTANT POINT 14: Without fear or doubt, my programming became more effective. I was only visualising the end result and not worrying about the minor details or how I would get there.

After a while, my meditation changed and was becoming a little boring. I can remember sitting in the front room of my house and as I was attempting to meditate, I seemed to get a lot of strange images coming into my mind. I could also hear the cars, the dogs, the children and everything else going on. After one month of doing this, I became annoyed. I decided I wasn't going to meditate anymore and I said to Judy, "I go in there to meditate and all I get is a lot of rubbish, I can't even remember any of it, and it's a waste of five minutes." "What do you mean?" Judy said "Five minutes you've been spending at least half an hour to an hour each day meditating!"

The next day, I asked Monomer if I could remember what all the strange images were going on in my mind. The result was something like this, I visualised an ocean liner which was actually Tuesday on the bottom of the ocean smoking a cigarette which became a goat upside down next to a house. This certainly did not make any sense to me and yet Monomer told me he was putting into my mind all of the symbols I needed. He said he had to put them in this way because I was logical and I would spend my time trying to analyse them, this was not necessary. I asked him how I was going to use them and he said "When the time comes the answers will come into your mind automatically."

He then said "The original symbols of your guides were no accident.

IMPORTANT POINT 15: Everything in this universe is connected."

He then went on to say "Although I (Monomer) appeared the way I did, it was to give you the information you needed to improve your thinking and your lifestyle, without realising it. You have learnt well, so we are moving you to the next phase."

"What is that I asked?"

Boy was I in for a surprise!

THE SURPRISE I DIDN'T SEE COMING

I was on a trip to New Zealand, the plane was delayed, and we landed at 2 AM. By the time I got to the motel it was 4 AM. I was to start my course at 8.30AM. I figured there was no point going to sleep. I decided to do some meditation work with Monomer. To my surprise instead of Monomer turning up a new Guide appeared. I asked her name she said it was Quintrex. Wow! What had happened? Was this because I was in New Zealand, although I had been here before many times and worked with Monomer? I asked her the question, "What does your name mean?" I was not expecting the answer I received. She said "You will need to find out yourself; walk around New Zealand's shopping centre and the answer will come."

At 6 o'clock I set out for the shopping centre. On the way I found the name Quintrex on a boat manufactured in New Zealand and also at the shopping centre a television set had the same name. I asked Quintrex which one she was referring to, she said "which was at the shopping centre." That was the television set." I said. Quintrex said "That is why I said the shopping centre, not on the way." This was a lesson for me.

IMPORTANT POINT 16: Pay full attention to what my Guide said.

Then Quintrex said I had to look at the symbol on the TV cabinet. There was a small symbol with four colours red, yellow, green and blue. As it was time for me to go to set up my course I didn't have time to ask the significance of the colours. When I returned to Australia at the first chance I had, I sat down to talk to Quintex about the symbol. She told me I had to research colours and I would understand. For the next six months, I looked into the significance of colours. This is what I found.

IMPORTANT POINT 17:
Red represents the physical things in this world.
Orange represents the emotions.
Yellow is significant to our thoughts.
Green is a symbol of peace.
Blue is related to relationships and love.
Purple indicates our self-development.
Violet is universal understanding.

I now felt I had sufficient information to ask Quintrex about her symbol. She said "The red in the symbol stood for the physical things that I needed in my world. The yellow represented the fact that I will always have streams of new thoughts. The green meant I would always be in a peaceful environment and the blue that I would have love in my life." I suddenly realised that Quinn means five and I asked "what was the fifth colour?" Quintrex said "It is white and white stands for knowledge.

IMPORTANT POINT 18: There are twelve phases of knowledge that man goes through on this earth."

Not understanding what she meant I asked if she could explain. The response I got is something that I had never connected before. She said "You have the:

The 12 labours of Hercules.
The 12 disciples of Jesus.
The 12 knights of the round table.
The 12 signs of the zodiac.
The 12 months in year.
All these have the same personality groups.

IMPORTANT POINT 19: My Guide said, "The earth also goes through 12 phases,

We have just come out of Pisces, which is significant. This is why the symbol of the fish was used for the early church, the disciples were known as the Fishers of Men. We are now in the cycle of Aquarius and at this time they are pouring knowledge into the earth."

IMPORTANT POINT 20: My Guide also said that each individual person will go through 12 phases of learning.

I did not understand quite what she meant. It was to be revealed to me later. As you go through this book you will start to understand the significance of the twelve phases that you will go through on earth. And believe me it will be as great a surprise to you as it was to me.

I now had the seven colours and a lot of mixed up symbols in my head. What use was it, to me? Then Quintrex asked me to remember, I had been asked to select a scene I enjoyed in a course I attended many years before. My scene was, me sitting with my back against a tree. To my right there was a small river flowing from left to right. I used to stand up and walk towards the river and throw in three coloured pebbles. Then I would turn around and walk to the left, walk down a slight hill to where there was a wattle forest about half a kilometre square, which reminded me of a wattle forest on my uncle's farm. We used to catch cicadas. Then I walk into the right-hand corner and quickly came out because I was a little frightened. There was an old wooden horse drawn cart which was falling apart; this was not there when I entered the forest. I would touch the cart and then walk back out on to a green field. At this point my Guide said "You can now recognise all of the symbols within the visual image you have created." And to my surprise I did.

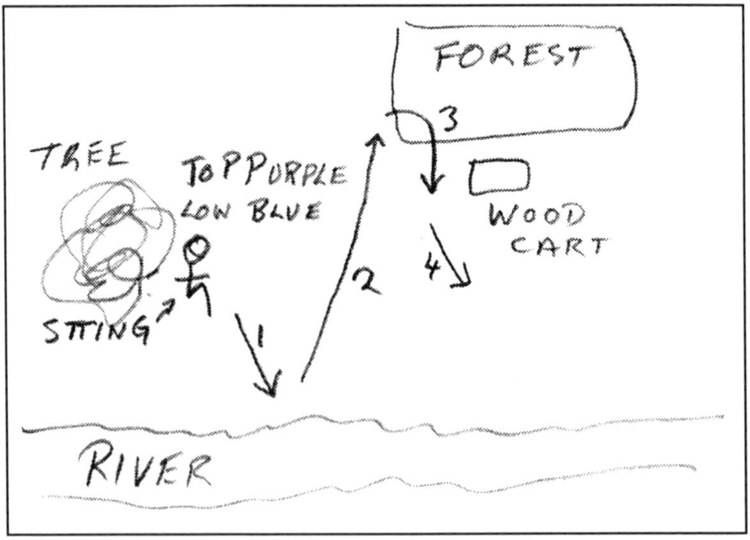

Before I explain what the symbols mean and what I learnt about myself all contained within the scene, I'm going to ask you to do an exercise.

Just relax, sit down and think of the most beautiful scene you could imagine. It can be a beach scene, a river scene, mountain scene, a forest scene any scene you like. Then take a pencil and paper and draw your image roughly. Note these points.

1: What is directly ahead?
2: What is to the left?
3: What is to the right?
4: What is behind you?
5: Are you sitting or standing?
6: The position of the sun?
7: Clothes you are wearing on top and lower parts of your body?
8: Are there any trees, rocks, houses, fences or animals?

I know you will probably tend to want to keep reading. I ask you to do your scene first, so you are not influenced in any way, before I tell you how to analyse your scene.

Then I will show you how to analyse your scene.

You will be surprised at the results.

So stop reading and draw your scene.

You have seen how I drew my scene just keep it simple.

1: What is directly ahead?
2: What is to the left?
3: What is to the right?
4: What is behind you?
5: Are you sitting or standing?
6: The position of the sun?
7: Clothes you are wearing on top and lower parts of your body?
8: Are there any trees, rocks, houses, fences or animals.

SCENE ANALYSIS

Scene analysis is fairly simple once you understand some of the basic principle.

Some people tell me the scene they have is one they know, or is a particular spot they enjoyed as a child. In other cases, people who draw scenes from their life, and say the original scene was slightly different. This is okay.

You can use total imagination and come up a scene that is not something you have ever experienced before. It does not make any difference. It is only an imaginary scene you are creating.

Everything in your scene is an indicator of your life now.

Once you have finished your drawing, you can start the analysis.

To do this use the symbols included in the next five pages.

There are more symbols in the back of the book.

MAIN SYMBOLS

OTHER symbols at back of book

Above scene:

Looking down from mountain or higher area, means you are **Observers or uninvolved** in the present situation.

At ground level:

Involved in what is going on around them.

Colours:	
Red:	Physical
Orange:	Emotional
Yellow:	Thoughts
Green:	Peace
Blue:	Love
Purple:	Self awareness
Violet:	Universal awareness
White:	Knowledge
Black:	Problems

Color of clothes:

Top:	Current learning or lesson
Lower:	You came in with or have experienced in the past.

DIRECTION

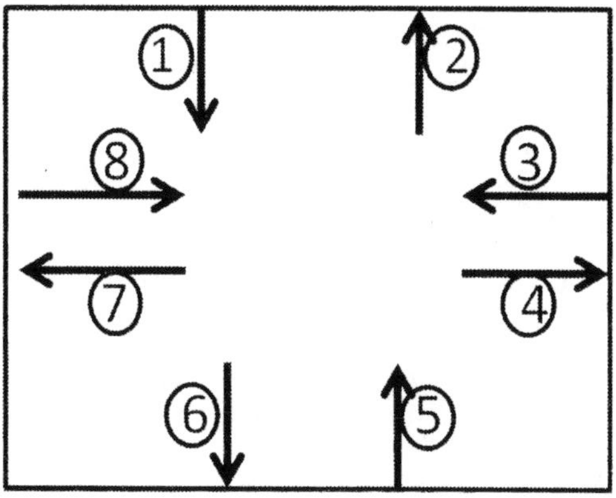

If you are moving in direction of arrow

Number 1	It is bringing it earlier in your life.
Number 2	It is moving it to later in your life.
Number 3	It is coming back from the past.
Number 4	It is moving into the past.
Number 5	It is coming from your early childhood.
Number 6	It is reminding you of your early life.
Number 7	It is delaying it to the future.
Number 8	It is bringing the future forward.

Flying above scene:

Indicates you are an observer and do not want to be involved in what's going on

Sitting: Not moving forward
On rock: The colours in the rock indicates area of problem.
On wood: How old. Indicates long term problem.

On plastic: What colour indicates area of problem. and is not a real problem. Fake or made up

Moon: A reflection and acceptance of someone else's attitude to god

People:

Left side: Right brain symbols (Intuitive)
People on the left side tells us you are tending to listen to their point of view on intuition ideas.

Right side: Left brain symbols (logic)
People on the right side tells us you are tending to listen to their point of view on logical ideas.

In front: Close to the person can either be helping or hindering progress of your goals.

Behind: Indications of the past. Relationships may be coming back into your life. Were they a good influence or a bad influence?

Position:

Left side: Right brain symbols (Intuitive)
Problems on the left side tells us you need to use intuition to resolve the issue.

Right side: Left brain symbols (logic)
Problems on the right side lets us know you need to use logic to resolve the issue

In front: Close to you are short term goals.
In the distance long term goals.
Any barriers indicate blockages to your goals.

Behind: Indications of the past.

Any barriers can indicate you are blocking out your childhood.

Standing:

	Moving or ready to move.
Sun:	**God** and your relationship
In front:	**Left** becoming spiritually aware
	Right moving towards religious beliefs.
Centre:	Shows balance between spiritual and religion.
Behind:	**Left** losing spiritual awareness.
	Right leaving behind religious beliefs.

Things coming from:

Left	is coming from your future
Right	returning from your past.

Things going to:

Left being delayed for the future.
Right going into the past.

Walking:

Already on the move
Moving to the left to a more spiritual awareness.
Moving to the right to a more logical lifestyle.

SAMPLE SCENES

Now look at some sample scenes. This will help you learn how to interpret scenes and enable you to alter scenes to achieve goals.

The first scene is my first scene, followed by the analyses and what I learnt about myself, then how I changed it.

Then four other examples with their analyses.

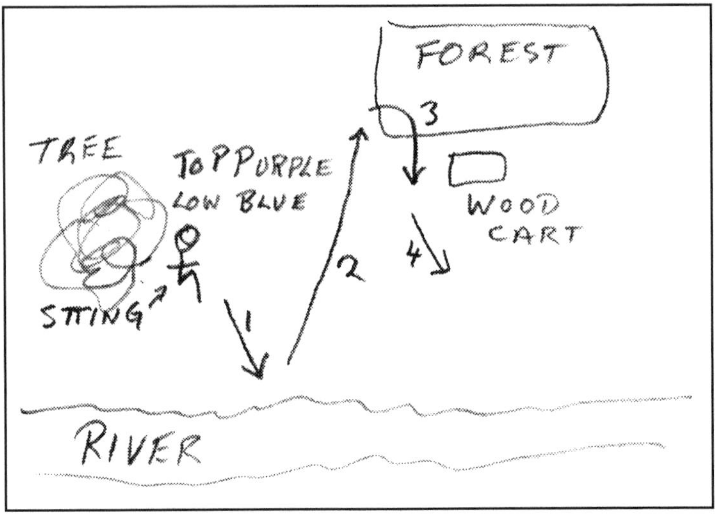

My Scene

In my scene I had my back against a tree, looking out over open green fields.

I was wearing purple shirt and blue shorts.

To my right was a river flowing from left to right.

I would stand up and throw three coloured rocks one red one orange and one yellow into the river.

Then walk down a slight hill to a wattle forest (Which is similar to one on my uncle's farm) where we used to catch cicadas. I would enter the right hand corner and only move a little way into the forest, and come out fairly quickly, because I was afraid of what might be in there.

When I came out, there was an old wooden horse cart on my right; this was not there when I entered the forest.

ANALYSIS OF MY SCENE

The fact that I was sitting meant I was at that time not moving, remaining for a short period of time.

I would then get up and walk to my right (logic side) and throw three rocks one red (physical) one orange (emotions) one yellow (thoughts) indicating that I was clearing my mind of outside distractions.

I would then proceed downhill to the forest where I would only go a little way into the forest (because I was afraid) this indicated that I was not getting fully involved in something that should be easy for me to handle. When I came out the old cart represented a long term problem.

When interpreted meant this, I was not fully going into any problems. (A little way into the forest)

When I came out I would come out with the same old long-term solutions. (Old wooden horse cart)

Once I realised this, I walked into the forest and wandered around and took my time to see what was there.

When I came out, the old wooden cart had gone. Indicating I was now looking deeper into my problems and coming up with new solutions.

The clothes I was wearing, purple shirt and blue shorts; this indicates I was working on self-development and came from a place with love.

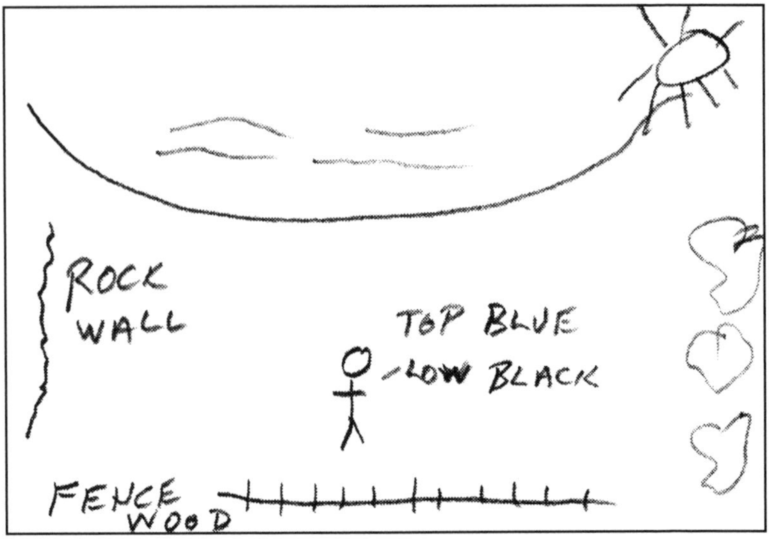

Scene 1

Beach scene looking forward towards fairly smooth water.

On the left there was a rock wall, the colours in the wall were dark orange and black.

On the right three trees.

Behind him was an old wooden fence.

He was standing.

The sun was in the top right hand corner.

He was wearing a blue top, lower black.

ANALYSIS OF SCENE 1

The water was fairly smooth; indicating this person did not like confrontation or arguments.

To his left was a rock wall. This indicates that he had problem on his intuitive side. The orange colour indicates it was emotional problems.

On the right-hand side he had three trees. This could indicate three different types of education or maybe different jobs where he has learned different skills.

Behind him was the old wooden fence, which shows he does not really want to discuss or be over involved in his childhood memories. This could indicate some long- term problems.

The fact that he is standing indicates that he is willing to move.

The sun being on the right tells us he was probably brought up in a religious family.

The clothes he is wearing, lower black, means he has come from problems or is still holding onto some he had earlier. The blue top indicates that he is here to learn about love and relationships.

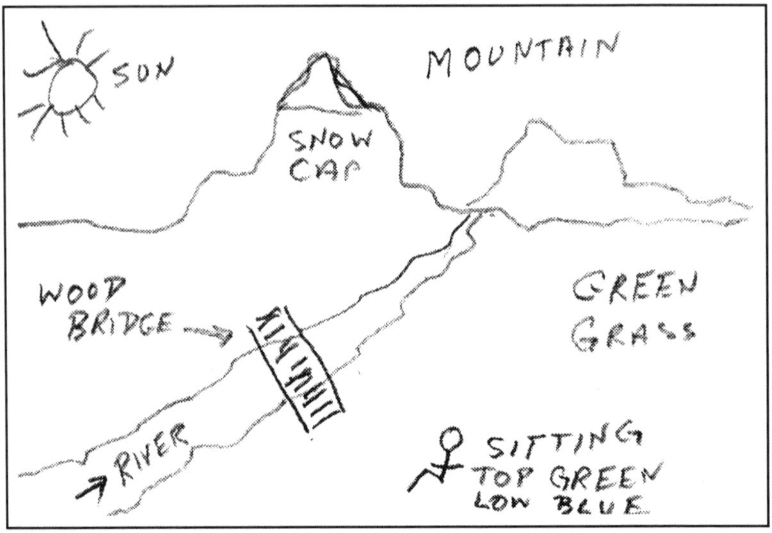

Scene 2

A field with a river and mountains.

Ahead of him a mountain with a snow-capped top.

To his left a river flowing towards the mountains.

A wooden bridge crossing to the left.

Green grass behind him and more grass to the right. He is sitting.

The sun is on the left hand corner ahead of him.

The lower part of his body is in blue, the top green.

ANALYSIS OF SCENE 2

The mountains, of which there are two, indicate he has two goals. The first one is snow-capped indicating, he is looking for knowledge first. The second is further in the future and looking for peace.

River flowing towards the mountains indicates that others he knows are also moving the same way.

As he is sitting a long term problem (the wooden bridge) is preventing him from getting to his goal of knowledge.

He has blue on the lower part of his body indicating he has come from a position of love, on the top is green showing that he wants to find peace.

The sun on the top left hand side indicates that he is more spiritual.

He could get up and walk on this side of the river and that would give him peace. It would not solve the long term problem or get him to his main objective, knowledge which is represented by the snow-capped mountain.

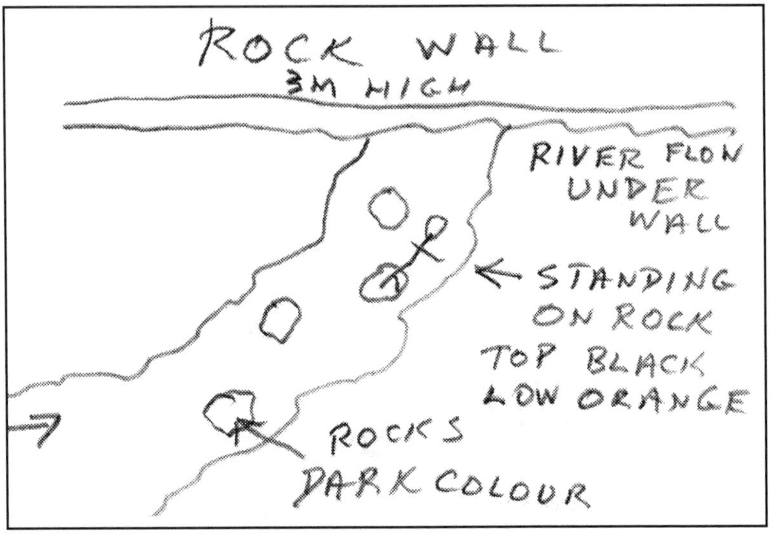

Scene 3

This was a valley with a river running from left to centre front.

Directly ahead was a rock wall about three metres high.

He was standing on a rock with water to the left and right.

He was moving from rock to rock upstream.

Behind him in the river were more rocks.

He couldn't see the sun.

The clothes he was wearing was black on the top and the lower section was orange.

ANALYSIS OF SCENE 3

This scene indicated he was moving from problem to problem.

Looking ahead he could only see a major obstacle as he could not see past the rock wall.

His clothes tell us he was having emotional problems.

The dark rocks represent relationships.

Every relationship he had, ended in a problem, because he was always looking for the problems and he was just jumping from one to another. As far as he could see there was a major situation coming up which he could not overcome.

He could not get around the rock wall.

I suggested he see if there was a way to climb over or go through. He found a cave which upon entering came out the other side of the wall to a clear open field with the sun directly ahead of him.

This indicated that once he had got past the short-term problem (represented by the rock wall) and stopped jumping from one relationship to another (by looking for problems) he would have a much smoother life.

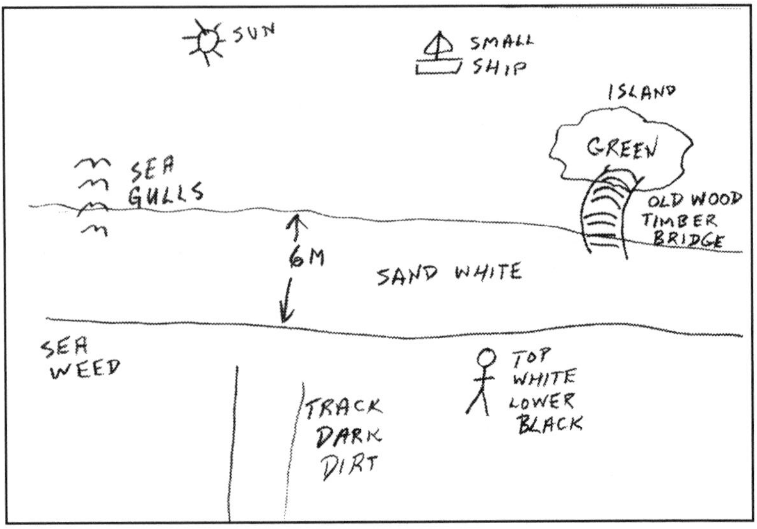

Scene 4

Looking forward, towards the water, which was in fact fairly rough.

Beach had white sand.

On the left there were four seagulls

On the right there was a green Island just offshore, with an old timber bridge from the beach to the island.

Behind her was a dark dirt track.

The sun was in the top left hand corner

She was wearing a beige top and the lower half was black

ANALYSIS OF SCENE 4

The water was fairly rough, with large waves, indicating she did not mind putting her ideas forward forcefully and had no difficulty dealing with aggressive people.

The white sand indicates there was a lot of knowledge around her and she needed to move forward to fully grasp the knowledge available to her, yet she was standing back.

To her left were four seagulls, indicating that she was very free-flowing on the intuitive side.

The island on her right showed she must use logic to get to the solution she needed. The old wooden bridge was a long-term problem that she needed to overcome.

The dirt track behind her shows there were problems in the past which she tends to still access.

The sun on the top left hand corner tells us that she was spiritual and has spiritual awareness

There was a small boat out in the distance, indicating that it would take her a long time before she could achieve her long-term goals.

SOLVING PROBLEMS

A barrier:

In front: such as a rock wall, trees, or cliff.

To help overcome the current problem, look for a pathway around the obstacle either left or right.

If you find a way round to the right you need to apply a logical solution.

If you find a way round, or a path to the left, you need to use your intuition.

You can fly up high and see what is beyond this barrier this will indicate what is for you waiting in the future.

Cliff:

In front: You are an observer. Fly or climb down to get involved.

Fences:

Blocking your way: Look for a gate to the left or right and then open the gate.

To the right: A logical solution will come.

To the left: Use your intuition to come up with a solution.

Rocks:

On the left or the right: If you are sitting on a rock, then look at the colour of the rock to determine the area of the problem.

Place your hand on the rock and as you do the problem will come to mind. As the problem is solved the rock will reduce in size till it disappears.

Surrounded by trees:

Not wanting to move from your present position. Look for a path in front to left or right hand side. Follow to see what is beyond the trees.

No long-term goals:

Beach scene: Bring a boat from the left into your scene.

Bring the boat ashore or fly out to the boat and stand on it to determine what your new goals could be.

No long-term goals:

Open land: Place a mountain in the distance.

Then fly to top of mountain and put your hands on it and see what comes into your mind.

Part 2

THE NEW ADVENTURE

Then the biggest surprise of all, something that changed my life's direction! A person, who I had helped became a friend, and one day turned up at my front door. He said "You are going to be a clinical hypnotherapist and a counsellor. I have enrolled you in both these courses and covered all costs."

It was rather a surprise to me, as I have no idea why he decided to enroll me.

IMPORTANT POINT 21: The strangest things often happen without us understanding quite why.

Once I completed the courses, I was not quite sure what to do with the information. Six months later I had not used any of the training. Then another friend asked would I see if I could help a friend? Now remember I was new to this and not sure what I was doing, I agreed reluctantly.

IMPORTANT POINT 22: Nothing happens by accident.

CASE 1
RELATIONSHIP PROBLEMS,

The client and his wife were having relationship problems. I decided to talk to them individually and see if I could help in any way. After a short discussion with the husband, I found out he had the belief that all women were not complete. He had been married and divorced on two previous occasions. This was his third wife.

Using a light form of hypnosis, I suggested he go to the time where the problem started. He started to describe a very comfortable warm place where he could not see anything. This made no sense to me so I asked him to go back a few months. He said he was standing with his father discussing the situation. I asked him what was being said, he told me his father said "It was too early and was not the right time for him to come."

I did not understand this, so I said go back to where you were again in the first place, then go forward twenty-four hours.

At this point he told me he had a headache and felt very strange, that the left hand side of his body felt slightly numb. This was frightening, not being sure what was happening, I said "go back to the original point." At this stage, the headache and numbness went.

"Let's go forward forty-eight hours." I was attempting to find out what was causing the headache and the numbness. He stated that all he could see were bright lights and people around him seem to be saying "It's a girl and it's not complete."

I asked him to go ahead another twenty-four hours and he said that the numbness had stopped, his head was clear and he did not seem to be particularly anywhere. Of course this made no sense to me, so I brought him out of the relaxed state, to see if we could discuss what happened and what he had seen.

During the discussion, I thought he may have gone back to a previous event he had witnessed. I asked him if he had a brother or sister or knew anyone in that situation. He said he was an only child.

Then my Guide suggested it was him in the womb and that he had been born a girl and died. (In my mind I asked my Guide "are you telling me this is a past life?" "Yes" replied my Guide. I suggested he go and talk to his mum and see if she could explain what had gone on. I told him I now believed he had had a sister who had been born and died twenty-four hours after birth

When he spoke to his mother and asked her if she had another child, (mind you she was now 80), she went pale white and said it was a family secret. "Thirteen years before you were born, we had a daughter, who was born with an incomplete brain and paralyzed down the left hand side; she died twenty four hours after birth." They had not intended to have him because they were too scared; unfortunately she had fallen pregnant during change of life.

IMPORTANT POINT 23: He had gone back to a past life where he was his own sister.

This was rather confusing to me because I was a person who did not believe in past lives. Yet he had described events he knew nothing about this had been kept as a family secret and never spoken about. Still he had described it all in full detail.

Of course if it was true the statement, I*t's a girl it's not complete,* had stuck in his mind.

IMPORTANT POINT 24: His past life was affecting his decisions.

In this lifetime he was actually picking women who were in his mind not complete, this was to maintain his belief system that girls were not complete.

This seemed way beyond my belief and I probably would have just put this down to an exception, or ignore it, believing it was some sort of fluke. Maybe I misinterpreted my Guide. Maybe someone had talked about it and he overheard. This would have been okay if it had not been for what happened when I talked to his wife.

CASE 2
SHE WAS GOING TO LEAVE HER HUSBAND

Her story was quite strange and was to change my view on many of my beliefs. She started off by telling me she was going to leave her husband and nothing I could say would stop it.

She was already seeing someone else, although at this point there was no sexual relationship.

At the time I did not believe in divorce and I felt I should discuss this with her. She was quite adamant she was leaving. Her husband treated her more like a daughter than a wife. In fact she called him mum because of his attitude and the way he acted toward her.

I decided to relax her and find out where this attitude came from. I told her to go back to the cause of the problem, as to why she wanted to leave.

Her story stopped me in my tracks. She described a situation where she was walking down a street towards a house; she was reluctant to go into this house. She said she was scared, I asked her why?

She didn't seem to know the reason. As she would not approach the house any closer I simply asked the question "Did you eventually go in?" She said "Yes." I asked her what happened when she came out. She said she was in a tremendous amount of pain. I asked "What had taken place?" She stated she had had an abortion. I asked her "Whose baby is it. She said "It's not my husband's." Then she made a strange statement she said "I have done this twice before." Not understanding what she meant, I asked her to explain. Said this was the second time she had been married and had affairs. (Now I knew she had not been married before in this life.) At this point I decided to try something different and out of the ordinary. I asked her to ask her Guide, which I had never done before, to explain what was meant by this statement. The Guide stated, through her, that she had two previous lives where she had relationships outside her marriage.

IMPORTANT POINT 25: She needed to learn to be loyal to her promises and her husband.

This took me way out of my comfort zone and I was not going to let the opportunity go. I asked her to ask her Guide, "Is the husband in this life the same one in the previous life?"

IMPORTANT POINT 26: She said "No, my husband in this life was my father in my previous life. He was the only one who would volunteer to come down and marry me this time."

This confused me a little because he had two marriages fail before this one. If he had not divorced the others how could he marry her? Nothing happens by accident!

So I went back to after the abortion and asked her to move forward one week where she informed me she had died from the abortion. Once again we were talking about past lives.

Not sure what to do next I decided to find out about the current boyfriend. I asked her to visualise him standing in front of her. When she did, I asked her to ask him and his Guide how he felt about the situation. The response astonished both of us and caught us off guard, He said "The moment she decided to leave her husband, I will leave her; this is part of her lesson."

At that point she sat up opened her eyes and said "This is all wrong. "I don't believe any of it. I'm going to go home and pack up, ring my boyfriend and leave my husband today."

The session stopped abruptly at that point. I said. "I didn't tell you anything you were the one that said it."

I felt terrible; I doubted myself and never expected to see her again.

One week later she rang and asked if she could see me.

When she arrived I was not sure what she wanted to do or what she expected from me. She sat down and started to talk. "Can I tell you what has happened this week, when I arrived home I picked up the phone and rang my boyfriend. When he answered, I said "I want to talk to you." As soon as he recognized my voice he said "Before you say anything, I have something to tell you, I am leaving today, going interstate and you're not coming with me." Then he hung up before I could say anything.

"I don't know what happened last week? I don't know how to take it? But what was predicted came true and I don't understand it!"

IMPORTANT POINT 27: It took a while for me to come to grips with what had happened. Past lives, talking to client's Guides through them, making statements they did not know or believe, predicting the future, divorce maybe okay, keeping promises, lessons, talking to people who weren't even in the room.

I had opened a Pandora's Box posing many questions that required new and different answers.

CASE 3
WOMAN WAS EXASPERATED WITH HER HUSBAND

Another example was a case of a husband and wife who told similar stories of past lives without knowledge of their partner's story.

This woman came to me, because she was becoming exasperated with her husband. She found, since he retired he was annoying her all the time. He was continually asking her questions and was not standing on his own feet, as she put it.

This of course was annoying her extremely, because he was around her twenty-four hours a day. She felt her space was being crowded and she needed time on her own. After a number of months of this, she decided the only solution was to leave him. This would give her space and cause him to learn to make decisions for himself.

For some reason, which she did not understand, although she had told him she was going to leave, she could not take the final step. As time went by she became more frustrated, and anger started to build.

Although she knew he loved her very much, would do anything for her, always wanted to be with her and please her. The fact was, he was crowding her. He said, to please her he would leave. Time went by and he was still there. She felt something had to be done because she was becoming more and more frustrated.

She came to me to find out what was stopping her from leaving and what should she do. She said if she did leave she felt she would be unhappy. She felt she needed to move and wanted her husband to make decisions on his own.

After relaxing her I asked her to go back to what was the cause of her problem.

She went back in time to where she was an old woman who lived much of her life on her own. She had lived a life of loneliness. As she felt the emotions and expressed the feelings of being on her own, tears were running down her face.

Then taking her past the end of that life, something I had not done before, I asked her what she had learned. She told us that she had learned about loneliness and being on her own and this was not a happy way to live. This was very obvious by the feelings coming through the woman, with tears running down her face as she sat in the chair.

I asked her Guide if in this life she needed to be on her own. She said "You can have time to yourself and at times be on your own, it is not necessary to break up or leave the relationship. This was not the way to go."

Hearing this we thought it was strange that we had gone to that particular life and not one related to her husband. I asked if there was a relationship, between her and her husband in another life. She immediately went to a time when she was in Rome.

IMPORTANT POINT 28: This time she had chosen to change sex and come down as a male.

As a Roman general in charge of a group of soldiers, the soldiers went into some form of arena in competition with other teams of soldiers. She did not seem to like the situation, because the soldiers she sent in to the arena were quite often injured and suffered a lot of pain. She was not happy with this although it was a way to show her soldiers were well trained and able to handle themselves. Obviously the arena they went into was some form of competition and entertainment.

I asked her to select one of the soldiers she knew well. She said there was one particular soldier who was a very close friend of hers and she felt really terrible about sending him into the arena. However he was quite willing to take on the challenge and probably suffer, because he would follow any orders she gave. He was the type of soldier who would have done anything to serve his commander and he did to the point where he sacrificed his life in the competition. This greatly affected her and she felt compassion for him, as she had, in her mind, destroyed her friend.

After this I asked to create a circle of universal light in her mind, then asked her to bring into the circle of light the old lady, the soldier, her Guide and herself. When they moved into the circle of light, she suddenly realised that this soldier was her current husband and in this lifetime he was under her control. I asked her Guide what was happening. She said "Her husband had come back in this life and was still asking questions and taking orders the same as he had in that previous life, because of the love and respect he had in the previous life when she was his commanding officer."

This of course gave her a greater understanding he still loved her very much, as he had expressed, and she acknowledged the closeness was there because of the previous life. She now knew why he was still relying on her to answer questions and give him directions.

The next week, when she came back, she said she had a greater understanding for her husband's position. Instead of being resentful when her husband asked her questions she seemed to understand the situation and did not feel so pressured. She also realised, if he was forced out on his own, when there was so much attachment to her, this could impact on him as it did on her, when she was the old lady.

She felt the relationship had improved dramatically. She told him about the life as an old lady and now she felt she did not need to go out on her own. She purposely did not mention how she was his commanding officer in Rome. She also told him that she felt if he had a session with me it would be beneficial. She wanted to see if he came up with the same situation because this would confirm her story and prove she was not making it up.

CASE 4
HER HUSBAND HAD A SCAR ON HIS SHOULDER

He decided to come and see me, not so much for the same problem. He had a scar on his shoulder from birth and it occasionally became very itchy and he would like to find out the reason behind it. Once he was relaxed I asked him to go back in time to find the cause of the scar.

He went back in time, to a time when he was an Indian boy aged 7. In that life he was looking for wisdom. Unfortunately, he was very passive. He tended to be abused by all the people around him. They took advantage of him and he was isolated because he did not want to be like the others who were strong hunters. He wanted to achieve understanding and knowledge. This of course led to many incidents in his life. The isolation increased and at forty he died of malnutrition.

Now at the time we could not understand why he had been given this life because it seemed so far from the question we had asked about the scar, although he had been bullied and others had taken things from him. Never the less there seem to be no point in the story that would have caused any form of scar.

I decided to go back to the original question and see if I could find what had caused the scar.

I asked a direct question about the scar on his shoulder.

This time he immediately went back to a time in Rome strangely enough the same era as his wife. I asked him what he was doing and he said he was using some type of powder or medicine he couldn't quite tell, a resin of some sort, to seal wounds on soldiers. I asked if he could tell me how these soldiers got the wounds.

He told me he used to be in a platoon of soldiers that took part in a competition where they rode horses in a sports arena. The horse racing was done under extreme conditions, where a number of groups of soldiers participated. The object was to knock over, push off, or get ahead of the other teams, using any means or methods necessary. If a member of a team finished first they would be declared the winners. It was a rather vicious and severe form of horse racing.

Realizing this may in fact be connected to the scar and his wife as a commander, I asked if he was just a soldier and why did he go into this type of games. He said he was just a soldier and that he went into the games because if they won they not only made their team look good, there was good prize money. He battled and fought mainly to be able to give money to the poor to buy bread.

At this point I said "How did you actually get the scar?

"He said he was in the arena when he was knocked from his horse. The orders were when you were knocked from your horse you stand up and try to dismount the opposition horsemen so your remaining horsemen could win. The opposition horsemen would just charge over any one who got in their way. Also the soldiers carried spears and swords to protect themselves and on this occasion, one of the soldiers speared him through the shoulder. He was taken out of the arena in very serious condition. He tried to get someone to apply some resin to stop the bleeding.

No was taking any notice of the particular wound in his shoulder and he died because the wound was still open and bleeding.

IMPORTANT POINT 29: He came back with the mark of the wound.

Every time he would feel tension or stress the wound would act up by getting itchy and he liked his wife to scratch or rub the birth mark so it would settle down.

IMPORTANT POINT 30: Then I asked him was the soldier giving food to the poor because of a previous lifetime. Was this why we had been shown the life where he died of starvation. He agreed that this was correct.

I asked what the connection was and what he needed to learn in this life.

IMPORTANT POINT 31: He said "He must bring forward the wisdom and the passiveness of the Indian together with the strength and the endurance of the soldier."

When we finished and we were just talking about what had taken place. Out of curiosity I asked him what he was doing as a job in this lifetime. He replied "I am a baker making bread and cakes."

When I met his wife on the next occasion I asked her about him as a baker. She said it's quite fascinating, he always takes pies or bread roles whenever he goes. He's now known as "the feeder of people." He gives friends bread and cakes all the time. If there is a party, he's always invited, because they know he will bring the pies and the cakes. So even in this life he is still carrying on the feeding of the people.

Now at that time he did not know that his wife was in fact his commander and this is why he asked her for help all the time. I suggested he and his wife should get together and talk about the sessions. So they could solve the problems they were having in their relationship.

We told him of his wife's past life. He asked if she was his commander, because she seems to have many of his characteristics. She said yes.

Then at my suggestion she said, "I promoted you to the same rank as me."

This sounded strange at the time and a month later she rang me to say he had changed. He was now making many decisions on his own and they were very happy together.

This is when I decided to be A Past-Life therapist.

From that day people just kept coming.

I never advertised and boy, did my life change. I now had access to many questions I had been asking all of my life.

What is life all about?

Is there an afterlife?

When we die are we punished or rewarded?

What actually goes on between lives?

And to my surprise, I could even find out about the future!

I also asked questions about the purpose of life.

How someone could bring information through from past lives to help themselves in this life.

What are the lessons all about?

Nothing was going to keep me from being involved as a past life therapist. I will share with you many of the different types of situations that people incur on this earth.

CASE 5
YOUNG GIRL BORN AUTISTIC

The next case that comes to mind is a woman who in a past life was born autistic. She lived in an upstairs room, a type of attic. The room was completely bare except for a fence which ran across the room protecting her from an open fireplace.

She was virtually a prisoner. Her parents were upset and embarrassed by her condition; they had isolated her from everyone. At the age of three all she wanted was her dolly.

I progressed her to the age of six and although she could understand me, she had difficulty interpreting what I was saying. I then took her to the age of eight. By this time she did not even seem to respond to my questions all she kept saying was she wanted her dolly.

One of the questions I asked her at this age was how she felt. She looked at me strangely and said she didn't understand. I took her back to the age of four and asked her could she answer the previous question? She looked at me and said "I now know what you meant although when I was at the age of eight it was if a bell was over the top of me and I couldn't comprehend or understand what you were talking about."

I asked her, "What age did you die?" She said "It was sometime after her eighth birthday. Her father had gone to get a doctor because she was sick, unfortunately on the trip to town he had an accident and was delayed overnight. She died of bronchitis."

IMPORTANT POINT 32: I asked her why anyone would choose such a life. She replied she had asked for a life without love.

Even this life had a purpose. It was for her to learn what a life is without love.

CASE 6
BORN DEAF, BLIND AND PARALYSED

I had another similar example where a young boy was born deaf, blind and paralysed. He could not move and could not communicate in any way. I asked him about that life because I could not understand why someone would choose to have all of those problems in one life. He told me it was one of the best lives he ever had. He said he learned to astral travel, to leave his body and travel all around the world discovering new concepts and ideas. This is what he asked for.

Again, here is a life we would consider incredibly horrible, yet the soul seems to see it as an opportunity to learn and experience. I also asked if this had been done for karmic reasons and he said, "No it was his choice." Consequently I learnt very quickly not to judge any situation or life people seemed to have. This taught me a very good lesson.

IMPORTANT POINT 33: I must not judge, condemn, or doubt people and what they do.

All of it is a learning process and when we judge we do not have all of the information necessary to make a correct or wise judgement. In life I do not judge anyone, for I obviously do not have all of the circumstances that created their situation.

CASE 7
BOY WHO WAS NOT HIMSELF

Another interesting case was a young boy who said he was not himself.

This sounds strange but let me explain. At about the age of 18 he was playing football and in a scrum which collapsed on him, he became unconscious. He was taken to hospital and on the way in the ambulance he died. They revived him but what happened between the time he died and when they revived him, a strange thing took place.

His soul left the body; he went through a tunnel ending in a large green park. Standing there was his twin brother who had died at birth.

His brother said to him, "You have totally stuffed up your life, you had every opportunity to be successful and yet all you have become is cranky, resentful and full of anger."

"It has been decided you are not going back again into that body. It has also been decided I will return and take your place." The next thing I remember I was in hospital in my brother's body.

Over the next few weeks' people said my face was changing, it was losing the anger I used to have. They said I seem to have learnt by my mistakes and were now more positive with a good outlook on life."

I knew of course they were comparing me with my brother who had been left in that field. I also knew I was not who they thought I was, I was in fact my dead twin brother.

IMPORTANT POINT 34: This is why I say to you "I am not my original self I am my brother."

There are many other interesting cases which challenged my thinking.

CASE 8
THE BOY WHO COULD NOT SLEEP

I had an experience with a young boy who hadn't slept comfortably for many years. When he went to bed he would wriggle and turn all night. He claimed that there was a woman screaming at him and a man who wanted him to get up and have a beer.

He had been seeing a psychologist who told him the voices in his head were imaginary and he should just stop listening to them.

This young boy had been on drugs. When I relaxed him, I asked his Guide what was the situation.

IMPORTANT POINT 35: His Guide said, "When people take drugs or pass out from alcohol, other entities can enter the body through the crown chakra.

In this boy's case, two previous souls had entered his body. I asked "Could I talk to the woman that was screaming." To my surprise she responded. "What do you want?" I asked her what her problem was. She said, she had overdosed on drugs and died in her sleep. She didn't know what to do or where to go, so she entered the boy's body and she was never going to let him sleep in case she died again. Every time the young boy tried to go to sleep she would start screaming. I told her she must leave the boy's body and go to the light, which is the gateway between earth and the afterlife. We brought down the light and sent her to it.

The second soul was a man, I asked him what he was doing. He said all he was trying to do was to get a drink of beer. He was in fact an alcoholic and died from alcohol poisoning. I told him he had to go to the light and he did as requested.

The next day, the father rang me and told me that it was the first night his son had a restful sleep, that when he woke up in the morning instead of the bedclothes being all over the place, they were almost as if he had just got in.

Obviously some of these **grey zone people** ***(I will explain them later. Page 85 Important Point 39)*** can in fact enter the bodies if people get drunk from alcohol or are on drugs and pass out. I found the simplest thing to do was to talk to them and send them to the light, this of course removes them from the person's body and they return to normal.

CASE 9
THE GIRL WHO LOSES WORDS

IMPORTANT POINT 36: People can bring through a problem from a past life.

This young woman said, every time she went to speak in a group and sometimes individually, as soon as she started to talk, she would forget what she was going to say.

Talking to her I could not see anything in this lifetime that could have created a situation such as this.

I relaxed her and took her back in time to a past life. The first image she recalled was walking down the street in a country town. She saw a woman on the other side of the road whom she had never met. In her mind she received one of her regular messages, not knowing what she meant. I asked her. She said, "She was continually getting words in her head, which were messages for other people." She then crossed the road and gave the woman the message. The woman was very thankful and said "You should keep using this gift, because it is obviously from God, you should be using it to help people." This was the first time someone had said it was a gift from God.

After consideration she decided to join the church and become a Nun, where she could help people with her gift. This worked well at first, then one day she told Mother Superior what had come into her mind. It was in connection to actions and attitudes of Mother Superior. Mother Superior was shocked that this nun knew this information, or received this type of message. So she transferred to her to the Benedictines Order where she was not allowed to speak. Unfortunately when she received messages for particular people in the order she would tell them. As punishment for talking, she was locked in a room without light and given one serving of rice per day for what she thought was about a week at first, then progressed to two weeks every time she made a mistake and talked.

We asked her Guide was this the problem that created the situation of her not being able to remember what she was about to say in this life.

He told us in this life every time she goes to speak her mind reverts back to the pain of being locked in the room, then the subconscious immediately shuts down what she is thinking to protect her. This seemed a very feasible and a logical answer.

A fortnight later the young woman rang me. She said the problem had gone completely and she was now able to express herself with ease. In fact now she has considered taking up public speaking as an interest, just to advance her ability to communicate.

She told me a joke.

In her convent there was a nun who came to maintain silence. In this particular order, you sleep on straw on the floor and have rice as your main meal. Each year you are allowed to express your feelings in two words. Normally nuns say such things as, "Praise God," "Enjoy silence," "Very happy," or even "Perfect life." After her first year of service she lay on the floor, as was the tradition to speak her two words and said "More food" and then she went back into a year of silence.

When a year past and it came time to speak again her words were "Clean straw" and then on her third year she said "I quit." Now the Father who was overseeing her progress and listens to her communications said "I'm glad because all you've ever done since you've been here is complain."

CASE 10
SHE HAS A FEAR OF FLYING.

A woman from New Zealand who had flown to Australia two years before, for some reason she has developed a fear of flying. She wants to know how to overcome it.

Under hypnosis we were first shown a happy life where she was a male named Paul. She was told by her Guide that this was a good time in Paul's life. When we asked if we needed any more information her Guide said we would come back to Paul later.

He then took us to a time in Rome where she was now a male named Simon in his late fifties. Simon was in charge of a gladiator and he had given orders which sent the gladiator, who was aged about twenty four, into battle. In the encounter the gladiator was killed. Simon felt this was unfair and gave up controlling gladiators and left to live in a cave.

Then it was back to Paul's life and at the age of twenty four he got his pilot license and because of the war became a fighter pilot. Paul was ordered into battle and during one of the battles, which was a total disaster, he was seriously injured. This created a great fear of flying.

The conclusion was she as Simon had ordered her gladiator into battle against her will. This created major problems in the life of Paul (the pilot), where he was ordered to go into battle, against his will which created the fear of flying.

In this life she is now in Australia and needs to fly home to New Zealand. It's interesting because she flew over before she was twenty two, when there was no fear.

Because of the life of the gladiator creating a fear of giving orders and Paul's life where she developed a fear of flying, the fear manifested at the same age as the gladiator and Paul. Now she has to order herself to take the flight. This of course is the karmic turn around. She is not ordering some-one else; she is ordering herself to fly.

CASE 11
WOULD NOT TALK TO MOTHER

This woman came to me because her mother was trying to contact her and she felt she did not want any contact. She did not know why. She told me she had rejected her mother right from birth. She said she had never had a good relationship with her and was more prone to talk to her father. She wanted to know whether there was something that took place early in her life that would have created the situation.

Under hypnosis, she went back to her conception and informed me that although she was connected, she did not fully enter the body of the child till it was quite mature, at about eight months in the womb. Even then she tended to only visit going in and out observing it from the outside then from the inside. She remembers one time when she was in the womb hearing her mother arguing with the father about her upcoming birth. Her mother said she did not want this child and continually said she was not happy about the birth, feeling it was not a good thing at this point in time. At that time, the child decided to reject the mother.

The moment she was born, she rejected any affection or attention by the mother, even down to refusing to breastfeed and finally had to be put on the bottle. As the child grew she continued to carry out the rejection through the early years, the teen years and into adulthood. Even though she had no conscious memory she could not accept her mother.

IMPORTANT POINT 37: Under hypnosis she could quote what was said word for word, even though at that stage she was in the womb.

At the end of the session she decided she would go and have a talk and see exactly what had happened.

She rang the next week telling me she had met her mother on Friday night. She was surprised at what took place. They talked till late in the night, all day Saturday and most of Sunday. They resolved all the issues that have gone on through the years. Her mother explained to her how, at the time the father was out of work and they did not have much money. She was not rejecting her, it's just at that time she did not feel they could give the child all the things she would need in the early stages of her life.

They talked about how her mum was upset because the child seemed not to want to be with her.

The woman rang me again a couple of months later to say that she was amazed at the character and strength of her mother that they had now become best friends. She felt all the years of refusing to talk to her mother had wasted a good and happy relationship.

CASE 12
THE GHOST WHISPERER

On a number of occasions people came to me because they could not sleep. They said their room was full of people at night time who kept talking to them and keeping them awake. I realised these people were in fact what we refer to as Ghost Whisperers.

People who have died and do not know they are dead maybe because they don't believe in an afterlife or God. They can enter what is referred to as the grey zone and then spend many years going over and over their situation not knowing what's going on.

Then for some strange reason they find a particular person can hear and see them, so they hang around in the hope they can find out what is happening.

IMPORTANT POINT 38: Ghost whisperers, are here to help these people caught in the grey zone to get back to the light and their past friends.

I teach them to relax. By using their imagination, develop a cave in their mind with a lift door on the left. They can use this cave to send people to the light. They enter their cave and tell the people that hang around them, they can only deal with one at a time. They then bring one person into their cave, talk about the situation they're in, find out when and how they died and direct them to the light which is through the door on the left-hand side.

CASE 13
THE GHOST WHISPERER AND THE BOY

For example one brought in by a ghost whisperer, was a young boy named John who had been walking through the forest and got lost. When she asked John what he was doing. John said "I am looking for my mother and father." She asked him "What year is it?" "1786" was his answer. She asked him to look around in the forest to see if he could find where he was sitting. John did and realising that he had died at night from exposure.

John said, "So I'm dead, what do I do now?" She told him to come into the cave and stand in front of the lift door, when it opened his mother and father would be standing there. John did as requested and when the door opened there were his parents. They said "You were lost in the forest and died, we have now found you, we are so glad please come with us into the light." John went through the door happy to be re-joined with his parents.

The ghost whisperer then went on to bring others in and release them from their eternal wandering. They found that instead of everyone being in the room chatting at once, people just came one at a time.

IMPORTANT POINT 39: The more I delved into this the more I understood that people who die suddenly and do not have strong beliefs or have no belief in a hereafter, can often get stuck in this grey zone.

CASE 14
ARM AND SHOULDER PROBLEMS

There were many cases where people had been affected by events from their past lives. I will give you some example cases, as they took place. The first one is Tony then we will look at Ann, which will give you a fuller understanding into the process of past life therapy.

In his life he had been through many different phases, divorce, and other problems. He suffered asthma as a child and it lasted till the day his father died then the asthma went. He realised it was psychological.

When he came to me his right arm was numb and he had a bad shoulder. He had tried a chiropractor, acupuncture and other physical things including pills and now he wanted to try a mental technique.

In the session, Tony went back to a young boy about six years old named Tom with a white toga and gold shoes. He was out in the field looking at the horses. When we asked why this was shown to us, they said it was because there were some good times happy times. He was able to talk to animals. Then later in life when responsibility became necessary he had to forget all that and become like others. To him this was a controlling factor and annoyed him greatly.

When he came into his next life he was named Harry. He came back as a motorbike rider who was out of the ordinary. We first met him in a storm water channel riding down the water into the dam. He tended to do many dangerous things where he would lose control.

He obviously rebelled against all authority. He did not finish school and became lonely. He was what you would call a risk taker. Unfortunately because he was such a risk taker, at the age of 20 he killed himself in a motorbike accident.

This is the actual session with Tony. We start part-way through the session. I am talking to Harry and his Guide named Derek about the arm and shoulder problems.

I will put my questions in this type face
The client's answers in this type face

Robert
Ask your Guide to take us to what we
need to be aware of in this scene.

I'm not sure. I keep walking and keep looking.
Maybe there are some older people there. I am
exploring on my own. To follow my own course

Do you know what you're trying to achieve
by following your own course?

No I don't know. I only want to be myself and not somebody else.

Is there a reason for this?

I'm the only one that has to understand and I don't have
to be responsible to anyone else. It's to be who you really
are rather than what other people want you to be.

Do you tend to resist being like others. Do you tend to automatically rebel against what others tell you to do?

At a deep level yes, not on the surface.

Do you think that's holding you back?

It could be I don't know if it is

Ask your Guide if that's why the arm is affected. Is it you trying to resist and hanging on for grim death?

Yes, that's it.

Hanging on so hard it's making your arm go numb?

That's right

And you are taking on the burden all the time because the burden is not to be like someone else?

That's right, that's what it is. You got it.

Does that make sense to you?

Yes. I can feel the arm changing it's a tension
it's holding on that's the word, tension

Can you forgive yourself for holding on and just let go?

Could you see how Tom could talk to the animals? Tom had his own individuality and he lost that because he had to take on responsibility and needed to be like everybody else.

Absolutely

He stopped being himself. Now you can let that go?

Yes

Tell Tom. I do not need that in this life

Yes

Then we will go and see Harry where he was taking on all the adventures and often losing control and that scared him a little because he really didn't know where he was going to end up. He was going to do whatever he wanted to do and this didn't help him as he took too many risks.

I understand.

And when you came into this life, you are hanging on to total control. You had to keep control. You feel if you let go you would take too many risks.

I want you to ask your Guide how Harry died.

Motorbike accident at 20

Can you understand when there's no control and no discipline and no responsibility, it can get out of hand.

Yes

You came into this life; you said something like, you are scared you might do something like that again.

You have been hanging on for grim death with all that tension in your arm hanging on to yourself

Yes

You can let all that go now. You do not need this anymore. You can change and be relaxed, calm and still be yourself in a much more effective way.

Now we're going to take all of the tension out of the arm and shoulder and you'll feel it returned to normal. How does that feel?

It's amazing how much better it is. Thank you.

PEOPLE COME BACK YET END UP REPEATING THE PROBLEM

Sometimes a person comes into a new life to solve particular problems or beliefs they have brought from a previous life. They were given alternatives to put into effect, yet sometimes they have such strong beliefs from their previous life it causes them to repeat the problem to confirm their old belief.

Pam is a typical example of someone who brings forward the belief system from a past life, continuing to make the same mistake by actually selecting people who will confirm her old belief.

Logic should tell Pam she should choose someone who is faithful and not someone who has been unfaithful to his wife by having an affair with her. Yet to confirm her belief, her mind allows her to think on this occasion an unfaithful man will change, because he loves her and not his previous wife. It seems quite obvious if a married man has an affair, and then leaves his wife to marry his mistress; he will not suddenly change. Obviously if he was unfaithful to his previous wife, what is to stop him doing the same again?

They are both here to learn and change and in this case it appears neither has.

CASE 15
ALL MEN ARE UNTRUSTWORTHY

I start by asking Pam to describe a scene. It was a beach scene. There was a crumbling down stone cottage on the right. A white house on the left with a bridge leading to it. She was standing on bridge heading, to the beach with yellow sand. She had a pink, mauve and yellow top, she had black on the lower part of her body.

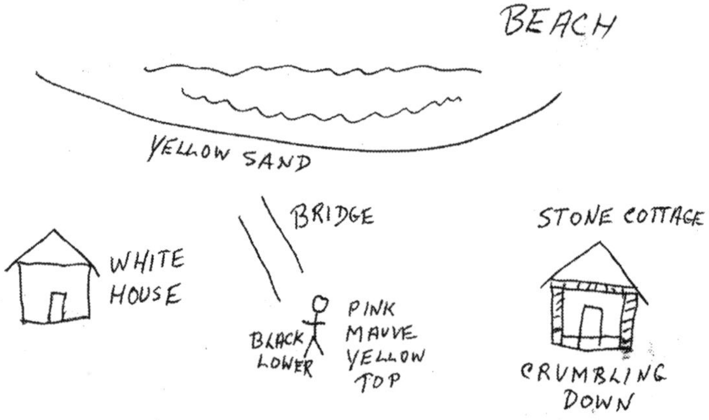

On the right hand side the crumbling old building, shows that her logic was falling apart. The bridge was stopping her from getting to the white house of knowledge. She had a pink, mauve and yellow top, showing she was learning about different things. She came from a negative life because she had black on the lower part of her body.

In her session we went first to when she was three. She was digging a dingy out from sand on a beach. She and her brother got into trouble receiving a beating. Her brother blamed her. This confirmed her belief, that all men tell lies all the time and they are untrustworthy.

Her father had married and named his daughter after a girl to whom he was engaged many years before, who had actually died. Her father was obsessed with this other woman. Her mother objected rejecting the daughter because she was named after the previous girlfriend.

Next we went back to find out what had happened in her first marriage. After a number of years, her husband became unfaithful; she was sad and finally left him. Her second marriage was to a man she had lived with for a number of years. He was in fact married to another woman in another country. Finally he got a divorce to marry her and confirmed her beliefs that men are unfaithful by being unfaithful to his previous wife.

We went back to find out why she believed men were unfaithful and kept choosing this type of partner. In a previous life, she was a nun named Maria and the scene that came into mind was a priest looking at one of the other nuns, he had removed her veil. Maria took her veil off parading past the priest who turned his

PAM'S SESSION

Again I will put my questions in this type face

and

the client's answers in this type face

Robert

Go back to the first time this problem arose
Tell me what you've got on your feet

Pam

Sand, standing in the sand

What clothes have you got on?

White flowing dress.

How old are you?

About three

What name do they call you by?

Simone

You will be able to recall everything that Simone knew at three years old when she was in that white dress. Simone what is going on around, as you're standing on the sand?

We're trying to get into the other dingy. It was buried in the sand on our fathers plantation in the Hebrides There's my younger brother, we got the boat out and there was a big hole in it

Tell me how you were feeling at that time?

Very happy!

What decisions were you making about life at that time when you were three years old when you were digging out that boat?

I was going to join my father, I followed him everywhere.

When you dug the boat out and it had a hole in it, how did that make you feel?

Didn't seem to worry us and we put it in the sea. It wasn't far off the beach

What happened?

We were seen doing it and we got the biggest bopping we ever got and I screamed. I will tell Daddy on them when he comes back. I told him and then he gave me a belting

So you got two how did that make you feel?

I was a bit cross with them and I cried and he took a handkerchief out and wiped my tears away, he said it was to teach me a lesson.

You are very happy when you found the boat. You put in the water and you got a beating for doing it?

We didn't realise it was sinking, of course we wouldn't have got far and we were quite safe, as far as we were concerned.

When you got that belting how did you feel about the world? I mean you felt quite safe at the time.

Yet you received two beating. How did you feel about that and what decisions did you make?

I wouldn't speak to my brother. I knew I was right and I knew I was wrong because we were not allowed to go in the water. We thought we'd be smart and we thought we were safe.... and it was my brother's idea.

Did you blame your brother?

He blamed me but I said "it was all your idea." I always got the beatings for him... from my dad. Not my mum. There's not much between my mother and me. I was rejected the moment I was born because of my name.

Because of your name?

My father was engaged when he was 25 and there was a difference between the families. He was engaged to a beautiful young lady. He went off to the First World War and for 18 months he didn't get any news. When he got back from the war he found out she had died. He was devastated and didn't get married till he was 45. When I was born he named me after the girl and when my mother found out what he'd done she rejected me and him. In fact the first time in my life she called me darling was on my 50th birthday, not realising it wasn't even my birthday. I am yet to hear my mother say she loves me and dad had passed away by then.

Is that all we need to know about that scene?

There's something else about what I am wearing.

Then tell me what you are wearing?

It's a little suit, got a bodice, shoulder straps, got little pants in it.

Asked why this is significant?

Because it was pink in colour

Now we want to go to the next important scene that you need to know about?

I'm walking down the aisle when I married my first husband and my father handed me a picture of himself and I looked at him and he was crying. But I said to him I would still be here for him and I was sad because I was leaving my father. My new husband was in the Navy and dad knew we would be moving around. We were married in 62 and in 69 we separated.

Why did that marriage fall apart?

I just couldn't take cruising with his mates and his unfaithfulness. One of his girlfriend's came knocking at my door one day, saying she'd come to see her husband because this was the address he'd given her. And she said she was pregnant again. So we had a good talk, then I packed my things, I called dad and he said come back to him.

Now we are going to go back before this time to find out why you choose men that are unfaithful. What are you trying to prove?

I'm dressed as a nun in a monastery with bells ringing.

How old are you and what is your name?

18 Maria

Maria what is going on in your life and how are you feeling?

Very attracted to the young priest.

What is the reason you became a nun?

To get away from the outside world, too much bitterness and too much sadness.

So you are basically running away from the world and yet you have become attracted to this priest.

And then I see the priest with another nun.

What do you mean you see him with another nun? In what way, emotionally involved?

Emotionally, he's taken her veil off and her hair is all down.

How does that make you feel?

I've taken my veil off and my hair is way down past my backside. She has nasty hair; mine is a deep rich auburn.

Why were you doing that?

I just walked straight past him and I could feel his eyes looking at me.

Was that good?

I felt satisfied

and then I never trusted men again.

What decision did you make about men? Has this affect all your relationships with men?

I never trusted them again. I don't believe them. Every ten words they say are crawling with lies.

They are always looking at someone else.

Always looking at someone else, rather than the one they are with.

Is that all we need to know about in this scene?

Yes

Let's look at this information.

When you were a nun, see how you lost confidence in men. When you paraded in front of the priest and he looked at you then you decided that men were untrustworthy.

Then when you were a three year old girl and dug up the boat your brother said it was your fault even though you knew it was his. This confirmed at the start of this life that men were untrustworthy and seem to lie all the time.

Consequently, you selected a husband that would betray you so you could maintain your belief system, that all men tell lies

Finally as an absolute proof, you had an affair with a married man, then married him, knowing that he would probably betray you, which of course he did; he betrayed his wife to marry you.

Now you have the final proof, all men are untrustworthy and it is not your fault.

I don't believe men and I keep proving it by the men I choose.

CASE 16
PARALLEL LIVES.

This case is very fascinating. It shows how someone can live parallel lives one life as a senator, the second life (at the same time), as the son of a tribal leader.

These two groups were about to go to war, against each other. He had a life on each side of the upcoming war. In both cases he was against the war and his parents were in favour of the war for different reasons.

You will notice when he starts his story he says he has different clothes on left and right side of his body, this was confusing, till my Guide told me he was describing parallel lives.

Again I put my questions in this type face
and
the client's answers in this type face

Robert
Look down at your feet and tell me what is on your feet.

Andrew
On the right foot is a good quality leather sandal and on the left foot a white cloth shoe with a burgundy tie. Two different shoes.

Just look at your clothes.

On the right side is just a creamy linen fairly loose weave, on the other side is a white robe with a burgundy trim which matches the white and burgundy on the shoes.

Can't make up your mind?

(*Then my guide said "He is describing parallel lives."*)

In a moment you will hear a name called.

Pedr P E D R.

How old is Pedr?

32

What is happening around Pedr?

It is a white marble meeting room with steps and a lot of men wearing the white robe with trim sitting around, like in an auditorium, a half circle like a senate gathering and someone standing in the middle.

And what's on the other side?

Like a village type of setting with camels and some mud or sandstone type of buildings, brown soil.

Let's look at the Senate room and what feelings do you get?

A little frustrated, not knowing which way to go, listening to both sides of the discussion.

A little confusion in your mind?

Someone standing in the middle of the room,
talking about declaring all-out war.

How do you feel about that?

I can see the reason that it needs to be, yet a stand needs
to be taken, when I think of the ramifications, death,
pestilence and everything else that goes with war.

Let the scene go on and tell me if they take
a vote and which way do you vote?

Not to go ahead with the war.

How many people are voting with you?

Not many probably a quarter of the group.

How does that make the others feel, the
ones had voted in favour of war?

Well this is what we normally do. I'm still a bit confused because
I can see both points of view. It's like a value judgement, a
conscience vote, the human thing versus the money thing.

Tell me this; does anyone in your group, that's the quarter
who voted against the war, change their mind?

A couple could well be persuade, because they are approached by
the other group and they do move across. Traitors, because the
war is about money and they can see they'll lose their trade.

When it's all over, I guess they obviously go to war.
Does that have a repercussion on you in any way?

I get stabbed in the back because I didn't agree with the majority and therefore four of them took me out.

Four came against you?

There is a raised marble pond, they stabbed me in the back. I fell forward and they pushed my head into the water.

What decision did you make about yourself at that point in time?

That it was the right thing to be doing.

And what decision did you make as they attacked you?

How unfair they created the war.

Out of curiosity did they win the war?

They won.

Have a look at the other side now, when you had the cream robe on how is Pedr feeling?

Well that's who the war was against.

And they are relatively peaceful dwellers who were trying to stand up for their rights.

And were you one of them at the same time?

Yes

So what happened to Pedr in that situation?

Well it was almost the same debate in that situation, except they wanted to wage war in defence, not run away.

How did you feel about that at that time? Should you have gone to war or should you have left?

Again I could see both sides and I did not want to run away but I was rather confused.

When they came what did you do?

I ended up joining in and I died.

How did you get killed?

With a spear.

What decision did you make before the battle started? Were you trying to talk people into it or out of war, or say they had no choice?

I was only quite young at that time.

What decision did you make about life at that time?

You can't win.

It wasn't a matter of choice it was a matter of have to? Now I want you to ask is there anything else we need to know?

Yes. We are going back to the left hand side, to the pond.

One of the people who killed me, is my now brother.

Your brother in this life, how does that make you feel?

Rejected, but mum who was a male was one of those people as well.

And was she on the side of going to war?

Yes

She rejected you there as well as your brother.
Why did they want to get rid of you?

Because I was an obstacle to them making money my mum controlled the Senate and I was a threat to her power. It's almost like she knew she was doing wrong but the power was more important, where with my brother I think he knew he shouldn't be doing it, but was persuaded by mum.

What type of role does your mum play in this life?

Subservient, but I think she has the power.

Even though she played a subservient role, can you understand how her thinking is coming through from the previous time?

Yes, and by me arriving in this life, I was going to affect her money situation again, she wanted to do her own thing, but by me arriving she couldn't.

If this is the case why did you come into this lifetime again associated with her?

An overwhelming sense of guilt from that other life, she knew in fact what she was doing was wrong and because she knew I was going to become a leader in the Senate, I was too vocal, articular and I was swaying to many people and was eroding the power that she had spent years creating.

Now when you came here as the third child in the family, many years after the first two, did she feel because she took your life before she had to give you life this time?

Yes. That was the only way to rid herself of the guilt.

Does that make sense to you?

Yes, I came into an area of marketing where I was using my voice again, maybe it wasn't a pleasant choice for her but I have to do it to get rid of her guilt.

She felt she was forced to do it and once you came in did her opinion change?

Yes, she really loved me; there was no doubt about that.

Did you let the rejection go, or did you keep it going yourself?

Yes. Because I had to battle that power issue and I felt I was sacrificing myself to help her with the karmic issue.

Now is there anything else we need to know?

Now there's a part dad plays in this as well. He was the leader of the tribe, he knew there was no choice and he didn't have any guilt in what he did because they had to fight.

What relationship was he to you?

I think I was his son and he thought I was weak because I didn't want to go to the battle because I was talking about other options rather than just go and draw swords.

I was doing the same thing there; I was speaking out against war and him. Yet when I died he had trouble excepting the loss in the light of his decision.

How was your dad, in this life?

He was generally very quiet and says very little.

Can we sum up what has happened in this previous life and how it has affected you in this life?

I had two lives simultaneously; two paths parallel paths, with me on both sides. My dad, as a leader of the tribe, lost his son in battle, when his son did not want to be involved. My mum a powerful senator on opposite side, who removed me as a young man and carried the guilt. Yet in this life both be drawn together by marriage and have me as a child. Which means enemies in one life came together as husband and wife in another life.

People reincarnate together to solve karmic situations. In some relationship where a husband is aggressive to his wife, in the next life it could be that the wife of the previous life becomes the aggressive husband and the husband of the previous life becomes the victim wife. This is so both learn what it's like to be the aggressor and the receiver. Eventually they may learn.

The universe is very clever as to how it attempts to solve problems. It is quite common for a husband and wife to come to earth in several lives in different roles, till they learn to solve all situations. When they went to the afterlife they would be taught how to handle it differently. Then they come down to test what they have learnt and how to put the solution into effect. They may decide to come down to help each other.

CASE 17
EVEN AFTER DEATH, WE LEARN

In this case we see where a child comes in for a **filler life, (see Page 131)** in the hope of helping the mother with her karma.

When the child dies in a car accident at the age of three, she looks down at her mother and observed the pain. This has such an emotional effect on the child, it affects the child's next life; she is so protective of her children she did not get on with her own life.

Again I will put my questions in this type face
the client's answers in this type face

Robert
Who do you see?

Client
A little girl about three years old named Patty

What's she wearing and what's going on around you?

A little pink and white dress she's drawing.

How does she feel as she's doing that drawing?

She's all right, her mummy is picking her up, and they are going in a car to the mountains. There's an accident, she gets killed and she's looking down on the accident.

How does she feel as she's looking down?

She wants to save her mum

And can she do anything about that?

No

How does that make her feel?

Not good

What year was this?

The seventies

How do they feel about life?

They were happy, they had Patty, when she died they went cold

What was she trying to teach them?

Passion and regret and her mum never got over it. And Patty couldn't get through to her mum.

Is she trying to help the family realise about loss and disappointment in the family? To lose someone you love very much. Teaching what it was like to lose someone?

Yes

Do we need to know any more about that scene?

Persecution, something about persecution.

Take us forward in time to show us what
she means by persecution?

Mum at the funeral is cross, bitter and the persecuted feeling that God would take a baby.

And how does that make the three year old feel as she watches?

I don't know, I am all right, going really cold, no love and I feel so bad.

Why did she have to do it, why did she have to move out and cause that? Was there's something in mum's Karma, something mum needed to experience and learn?

It was an important lesson for her mother. It also taught me as a soul to understand the grief and loss.

Can you ask the little girl for one piece of advice for this lifetime?

Be yourself

She asked the question "why me? Can you answer the question?

She says it was not a personal journey.

She wants to say something else to you at this time.

She says I was in denial.

Do you understand that?

No

How that has impounded on you in this life?

Oh my God my children. I realise I've used my kids as an excuse for not defining myself, not doing the things I want to do

Ask the little girl is the misery she saw in her mother the reason she made the decision she wanted to help others? She would sacrifice herself?

Because I caused so much pain.

Can you forgive yourself for that?

Yes

Tell your God "I accept forgiveness. I will no longer punish myself, it's just a soul journey."

Part 3

LIFE START TO FINISH.

Who am I and why did I come?

You need to consider looking at the wisdom of the universe.

Not knowledge or human logic.

If you look at the facts and make decisions on those facts, you are using human logic.

If you understand there is a reason for the situation and has a universal purpose.

Then you look behind the facts and the situation for the wisdom of the universe.

Only then will you discover the learning that you need to apply to your life.

BEFORE YOU COME TO EARTH

As a past life therapist, when I was dealing with clients I often ask their guides about:

The principles of life?

What this earth is all about?

Why do we come to earth?

What is the purpose of a particular life?

From these questions and answers I have developed my own theories. My hope is as you read this section of the book you will find it gives you new concepts and a greater understanding of life on earth.

You are an eternal being. What does that mean? It means you'll be around for a long time eternity,

How long is eternity?

What is the number of infinity?

YOUR CONNECTION TO THE SOURCE

IMPORTANT POINT 40: You are a part of the Universal Mind or God.

A small part is released, then it goes through a process of being given personality traits and this becomes your Higher Self. You are assigned a soul group, which numbers about forty-seven. From this group you will have brothers, sisters, husbands, wives cousins, and friends. As you progress some souls move out of your group.

From other groups you may choose father, mother, uncle, or neighbours. After some learning processes you have developed the higher-self sufficiently to send part of it to earth.

It appears souls do not work on the typical management structure as we do here on earth. Where orders are given and must be followed.

There are older, wiser souls with more experience; they seem to treat everyone as equal.

IMPORTANT POINT 41: Even the Council of Elders appears to only give advice.

Your guides also will not make decisions for you. They put up alternatives, even the schools of learning, only show you alternate ways to handle situations and show the outcomes. You are not told what or how to conduct your progress as a soul.

IMPORTANT POINT 42: you have total free will.

Souls seem to project different colours as they progress and are easily recognised.

Level 1 Souls are white with a tinge of pink.
Level 2 Souls are pale orange with a tinge of white.
Level 3 Souls are gold with a tinge of green.
Level 4 Souls are blue with a tinge of gold.
Level 5 Souls are blue with a tinge of purple.

In the afterlife, souls apparently appear as they do down here, and they do not seem to age.

It appears if one soul approaches another soul, they communicate telepathically. They project an image of who they were in a previous life relative to the other soul. If two souls look at the same soul they may see two different images according to how they remember the other soul in a previous life. Souls must have physical form and substance as a young girl was talking about between lives, said "she was riding a donkey."

These day's people take photos and find Orbs. According to some people they are souls, I cannot confirm this because these Orbs were not something I asked about, although they seem to contain the colours of the different level souls.

Then you can come to earth. The choice is yours. Before you come to earth you decide on your goals. Then a meeting is held with the Council of Elders, to discuss your ideas and goals. They then advise you on the best way to achieve your objectives. Your Guide also, gives you some advice.

You think it will be great fun to come down to earth. You believe you have it all under control. You will come to earth for the excitement and the joy. This is not considered to be a horrible place; it is a place of learning.

IMPORTANT POINT 43: You only send a part of your soul.

Anywhere between 20% and 80% depending on how much you need to achieve the objectives you set for yourself.

IMPORTANT POINT 44: Your higher-self will remain behind to monitor what's happening on Earth.

IMPORTANT POINT 45: After your life on Earth you return and go to school, where you review your past life.

What you did right and where you have sinned. The word Sin is a word used in archery and it means that you have missed your target. This is a target or lesson you set for yourself in this life or previous lives. When you miss the target you will be given information on alternate ways to solve the situation and their results.

IMPORTANT POINT 46: There is no judgement.

This is a learning process where you are given a number of options. Then you may choose to come again to solve the situation.

Before you return to earth you decide your goals and, once again a meeting is held with the Council of Elders and again you discus your new ideas and goals.

IMPORTANT POINT 47: Then you decide if you are to be male or female.

On most occasions, you will chose to be the same sex 75% of the time. Sometimes you will choose the opposite sex, if you want a different perspective on a particular situation. The Council of Elders then advise you on the best way to achieve your objectives. Then they present these recommendations to you and your Guide.

IMPORTANT POINT 48: Then your Guide gives you a choice of one of three new bodies or should I say lives.

You do this by sitting in a room where there are video screens around you. You see events from the possible lives, so you can make a choice.

IMPORTANT POINT 49: You are given the options to choose your parents.

You may also get to talk to the Higher Self of your selected parents. This is so you understand their views and opinions, and then they agree to display certain characteristics towards you.

Each of these lives is perfect for you to test your learning. Remember it is entirely your choice. You can even decide not to come at that stage.

Some souls come back very quickly within months or even weeks. Some souls even come back in a new life before the current life is finished. This means they have two parts of the soul on this planet at the same time. Then again you may choose not to come for a long time.

IMPORTANT POINT 50: If you chose to come you will be given event markers.

These are points in time where certain events will take place, to show you that you are on course. I'm sure you're aware there are people who have said they saw someone for the first time and knew that was who they were going to marry. The triggers can be strange sometimes. I remember one case where a man saw a woman in one of those Arabian style dresses at a costume party; this was not her normal style of dress, yet that was his trigger.

Also one of my friends said he would marry a girl who was tall and with long blonde hair. He did this. We have to remember that the only girls he was attracted to had long blonde hair.

This was obviously a code or a situation from a past life event that created this attraction. First he was not looking at the personality he was looking at whether the girl had long blonde hair. Now he may have had a fear of girls that had dark hair. When his first marriage collapsed, ending in divorce. He then married a girl with long blonde hair.

Triggers come in many different ways. It could be as simple as someone giving you a piece of advice if you are off track, or someone congratulating you on achieving a goal you set for yourself. Sometimes to keep you on track, people you come in to contact may make a very simple statement or take an action which changes your life, as my friend who enrolled me to be a hypnotherapist and counsellor.

WHEN YOU COME TO EARTH:

IMPORTANT POINT 51:

1: ***What you make of your life is up to you.***
2: ***There is no better place to test your learning.***
3: ***You receive the body you chose.***
4: ***You will be presented with lessons.***
These are the lessons you asked to learn, when you came to earth.
5: ***There are no mistakes only lessons.***
6: ***The lessons are repeated until learned.***
If you have a problem more than three times, it's probably one of your lessons.
7: ***Lessons do not end.***
If you complete what you've come for, you will probably move on to new lessons.
8: ***Others are only mirrors to you.***
When I say mirrors to you I mean what they do and say is a message to you for your learning.

When a situation takes place, be aware of how you react. If a negative situation comes up, it is probably for your learning. No situation comes into your life unless you make a request. The problem is how you react.

9: ***All the answers to any problem you receive are inside you.***
Because remember when you were in the afterlife you were given the answers. Now it is the time to see how much you've actually learnt and how much you know at a soul level.

10: ***YOU WILL FORGET ALL THIS AT BIRTH.***
If you have learned all of the answers before you come to earth. Then you forget the answers when you arrive why would you bother to come?

The reason is simple. Everything you've learned and studied before you come into a new life was to help you solve problems. You've gone through a number of experiences and alternative solutions also the advice of Council of Elders and your Guide. All that remains is inside you, as part of you and your soul.

Now you can test the difference between what you've been taught and what you've learned. Often when we are taught things we believe yet this does not mean we know them to be true, or will apply them when the time comes to take action.

Also, if you knew what was to come there would be no emotional reaction. You would think I know what that is, I knew it was coming and the emotional reaction you need to experience and confirm your learning would not take place. As with the case of the woman believed all men were liars and then only attracted to married men. This was a decision she came to change. Even though the problem may become very obvious to her, it does not mean she carries out what she was taught. You always have free will.

(Case Number 15 Page 92)

IMPORTANT POINT 52: The earth is designed to help you.

It is designed so you can learn through emotions. This earth is a planet of emotions. The emotions we feel are either love or fear.

IMPORTANT POINT 53: The main law on earth is the law of attraction. The "Law of Attraction" means like attracts like.

IMPORTANT POINT 54: Everything on earth is a reflection to you and your knowing.

In other words when a situation occurs which you have requested or programmed, sometimes by accident, you must look at how you react. Everything that happens in life has a purpose on earth

IMPORTANT POINT 55: All things are symbols to help you learn about yourself.

Every event that comes into your life has a message. There's good news and the best news. The good news is there is no better place than earth to learn because, there are no mistakes only lessons.

Remember you are testing what you have learned what you believe or know and the best news is you get to repeat the lesson again and again and again, with a twist until it is learned.

When things are going right and you feel good, you are on track. When things go wrong and you feel you are having difficulty handling the situation, you are moving away from your Higher Self and your objectives.

As you learn through experience and through handling situations, hopefully you come up with answers you have already been taught. This expands your soul and proves you have learnt.

Sometimes there are habits you bring down that need to change. Habits that have become part of your soul and are no longer necessary.

Sometimes you will program emotional upsets into your life, before you come, generally before the age of thirteen. These are often triggered by visual or auditory means to remind you of your life's objectives.

EXPLAIN KARMA.

At this point I would like to explain my perception of Karma.

IMPORTANT POINT 56: Karma is not a punishment, it is an attitude the person holds and can transfer from life to life.

If someone thinks they have done something wrong and deserve punishment and believe bad things will happen, then they will. If people think they are victims they will perpetuate the victim status and blame Karma.

People think karma is always from past lives yet this is not necessarily true, you can create karma in your current life. Statements like "It's too good to be true", "I knew it would not last" and "It always goes wrong" are typical statements that manifest what people say is Karma.

Karma works both ways, think fear you get fear, think love you get love. You get what you concentrate on.

Sometimes people get sick they say "what have I done to get this bad Karma?" It has nothing to do with what they have done; it is what they are thinking. **(See Important Point 8 Page 17)**

IMPORTANT POINT 57: Karma as you think, you receive.

YOU COME TO EARTH.

What you make of your life is up to you.

IMPORTANT POINT 58: You are still connected to the Higher Self by your emotions.

Some children remember past lives up to or about the age of seven. Others are talked out of the knowledge by family and friends.

There are many things that may influence this life and there are many combinations. Let's look at some of the factors.

A SHORT LIFE

Anger can sometimes stop souls coming in. One guy came to me and said, he had had a twin who died at birth. They wanted to be together in this life. Unfortunately the brother had so much anger that the anger destroyed his liver preventing him from being born until the anger is eased through learning in the afterlife. We found that quite often when a child is born with jaundice it is an indication they have gone out with a small amount of anger.

Earlier in the book **(Case 1 Page 52).** The young boy who came to earth as a girl and only had half a brain and paralysed, only survives twenty-four hours. This was karma for the family, not the child.

There is a case of a child who came to earth to be with a particular mother and not the current father. At the age of seven the daughter was killed in an accident. This caused so much friction in the family the husband left. The wife remarried and had a child. The same soul came down, this time to the correct parents.

Another case was a young girl who came down to be with a particular woman, she had been with before. She decided she would marry this woman's son so she could be with the woman. She spent more time with the woman than she did with the son. He was the only means to get to the person she wanted to be with. The young girl was unfortunately killed in a car accident.

The woman came to me to find out why the girl had died at the age of 18. We were told by her Guide the young girl was needed elsewhere and the boy was to marry someone else.

This leads us to a life which is known as a **filler life**. For example a couple may need to have the experience of losing a child. Children are sometimes abused and die early. The child actually comes knowing they will not be here for long, generally before the age of thirteen. They come in and go out to assist the parents with family karma. Also other children in the family may need the lesson of losing a sibling. It could also be karma of the child, the child needs to come in and go out early as part of its lesson. It may be the child needs to experience a different attitude, family or culture which they may need to have, or understand, so they come in quickly, experience it then move out.

I asked my teacher the question during one session why do people come in and overdose on drugs. He said this is karma. A lot of people who were coming in at that stage (1970 1980) were in fact coming back for the first time since they had lived in the time of Atlantis. They had not been on earth since then. Atlantis was a highly technical society, therefore they did not want to come back into earth until it was technically able to challenge and support them. For example, they would not enjoy a new life if they had come in in the Middle Ages. The problem was, the Masters who ran Atlantis, used drug to control their slaves and servants. When a child was born it was given drugs, that way the child could not leave the service of the Master and must do what they are told, otherwise they would go through withdrawal. The Master had many people they kept on drugs and in that way they maintained control. At the age of forty-seven, people were considered to be old and inefficient; they couldn't do their jobs, so the masters would overdose them and they would die.

What is happening now is these Masters are returning to earth. The first thing that happens is they end up on drugs, which is their karma. They overdose themselves and die at around the age of forty-seven. What comes around goes around. Karma is not punishment; karma is an awareness of what you put out comes back.

It's very hard in all these cases to judge, because we do not understand the full circumstances or situations of this young child or person who has a short life.

A LONG LIFE

If you have completed the goals you set for yourself before you came to earth you can stay and move onto new goals. If there is some characteristic you needed to change or something you need to learn. It may take longer than you expected and in some cases it may even be you need to be older and more mature to be able to experience the situation. Once you solve it you can live the experience longer.

It can also be family karma that you may have to remain longer to fix things in the family. You may have to become the patriarch or matriarch to be able to influence a certain situation. It may be a problem with your children or a friend you need to be here to give advice. You may have come to earth to help someone at a particular point in their life.

MALE OR FEMALE

Women and men think differently. Most souls come down the same sex 75% of the time. They may come down as the opposite sex to understand a different perspective and different way of thinking.

Unfortunately what often happens when some-one comes down as the opposite sex they still show many of the characteristics they had previously. Souls who normally come to earth as a woman, and chose to come as a man tend to be slightly effeminate. Souls who normally come to earth as a man then come as a woman tend to be slightly butch. Souls bring the characteristics with them. Remember they do this to perceive the other point of view in a particular situation.

One particular case of an estate agent who was normally a male, came to earth as a female in an attempt to understand a particular situation. The difficulty was she always dressed very masculine; she was forceful and very logical in her approach. She was having a lot of trouble softening her personality and being more intuitive to fit within the role of the female.

RICH OR POOR

To have or not have money is a symbol of your attitude toward money. Let me explain something about money if you are envious of people who have money you will probably have money problems. If you think some people have more money than they deserve and you haven't, the answer is because you have the wrong attitude to money. Some people think money is the root of all evil, or only bastards have money. They inevitably will have money problems.

When I visited a spiritual group many of them said "money is evil money is bad." Quite often many of them could not pay their own bills and barely had enough to survive. Why would anybody think God would want people to be poor? Another saying "poor people are happy." Money is just another measure of your attitude. Winning money with lotto can often be the worst thing that can happen.

I remember there was a guy who was an alcoholic and lived in Manly won $200,000. He gave $100,000 to his friend who used the money wisely and got out of the slums and the degradation and was enjoying life. However within three months the winner had drunk himself to death.

You can be poor because of karma or your attitude.

For souls who have learnt to handle money in previous lives, money seems to come to them automatically. Others may need to have money so there are no money worries and they can handle the lesson they came to learn

Are you here to learn about money and its role in life? You may have had a lot of money and wasted it.

You can be wealthy to learn about money or you can be poor to learn about money. Being poor at the start may teach you to treat money with care, and learn to understand attitudes you need to acquire money. If you have a life of wealth and you failed to use it properly, you may very well come into the next life with a lack of money.

ILLHEALTH

On the other hand you could choose ill health! Now this is strange, you can actually choose to be sick to learn about sickness. There was one particular case of a woman who had many lives where she had terminal illnesses. Why she choose sickness was the question. It turned out that she was a high level soul whose job it was to counsel people who had illnesses including terminal illnesses on earth and the illness had affected their soul. When the soul is affected by illness it creates a gap in the energy field of the soul. She counsels the soul back to perfect energy levels by sitting down and talking about the illness. She fully understands because she has experienced the illness herself. Then there is the soul who came down to experience the life so he could Astral travel **(Case 6 Page 69)**

When we look at someone with an illness, we can't judge them because we do not know all of the facts. We do not know if the illness is caused by attitude or it is a choice they made. What we need to do is help them and support them. People often ask why God allows sickness. God does not do it, our souls choice it for our learning. It is teaching us to have the right attitudes and the right approaches to life. The person chose that life for their benefit. It could be the person has had a life of good health and did not appreciate it.

There is one example in the Bible

v1. And as Jesus passed by, he saw a man who was blind from birth.

v2. And his disciples asked him, saying Master, who did sin, this man or his parents that he was born blind?

V3. Jesus answered. Neither hath this man sinned nor his parents; but that the works of God should be made manifest in him.

Well unless he had a previous life he it could not have been his sin, so obviously the disciples new about past lives. Maybe it was prearranged before he came to earth with Jesus to show his skills at healing or it indicates that in a previous life this man did not appreciate the beauty on earth. He was born blind, so he would not see the beauty. When Jesus heals him, suddenly he realises the beauty on earth because of the experience, he appreciated what he could now see.

Also the earlier case where a guy came to me with a scar on his shoulder **(Case 4 Page 62)** this was because when his soul went into the afterlife, it was not fully reenergised and came back with the scar, showing he had not completely released the problem.

WITH OR WITHOUT LOVE

(Case 5 Page 67) The autistic child who died at an early age was because she had come in to experience a life without love.

Then there are lives where a women came down, deciding not to get married did not have children and died lonely without family. **(Case 3 Page 58**)

This planet is designed with two emotions of love and fear.

They are there to help you learn about love and to teach you to love and to use love in all your decisions.

Fear controls you and you have no choice. Yet with love of yourself and others you have a choice.

POSITIVE OR NEGATIVE

Is the environment controlling you or are you controlling your environment?

Quite often we get a negative situation coming into our life and we make a judgement, this is right or wrong or good or bad. What we should be saying is, how do I use this situation to my advantage? How do I learn?

I came into this life with dyslexia when I went to my teacher asking why I had this problem, his answer was "If you had been able to read and write you would have become academic, if you became academic you wouldn't be learning what you're learning right now and you wouldn't know the things you need to teach."

I thought he was so right, I started psychology at University and went into the first lesson. The instructor asked "Does anyone know the difference between psychology and psychiatry?" No one appeared to want to answer, I volunteered an answer I said "psychiatry is something to do with the mind," he cut me off, and said "no, no, no that's wrong" and from that point on he never received another question answered from anyone. Everyone was too scared in case they were put down. I don't even remember the answer he gave, I had given him an answer which he could have said "I can understand where you're coming from and the real answer is." Then the situation would have encouraged the group to take the risk to answer. Not long after this during one of the lectures, someone asked a question about children coming in with different attitudes; "Was this from a past life?" His immediate answer was "No no, that's all rubbish." I left the class after that. Was it good luck or bad luck? Who knows? I do, nothing happens by accident.

Let me explain using a story about Jed

Jed lived on a country property a few miles out of town. One day a man came knocking on his front door and said "I have to get to town as soon as possible but my horse is very tired and needs water and food." Jed said "I have food and water if you want." Then the stranger said "I have to get to town do you have another horse." Jed said "The only horse I have is old and very reliable" The gentleman said "I will swap my horse with yours if you're willing." Jed looked at his horse, it was a beautiful thoroughbred. Jed said to the gentleman "Swap for now, I'll look after and feed your horse till you come back." The gentleman said "I am not coming back this way." So Jed ended up with a beautiful thoroughbred horse. Now the towns' people came out to see the new horse and said to Jed "What good luck." Then Jed in his old way said "Good luck, bad luck who knows" and said to himself, "Everything that happens in life has a purpose. The next week Jed went into town and bought a new saddle for the horse. That night they forgot to shut the gate and the horse bolted disappearing into the distance. Well the towns' people said "What bad luck" and Jed in his old ways said "Good luck, bad luck who knows." and said to himself, "Everything that happens in life has a purpose. The next day the horse returned and brought with it a whole lot of brumbies. The town's people said "What good luck," again Jed said "Good luck, bad luck who knows." and said to himself, "Everything that happens in life has a purpose. His son decided to break in some of the horses, on his second attempt he was thrown from the horse, crashed to the ground and broke his leg. Well the towns' people said "What bad luck," and once again Jed said "Good luck, bad luck who knows." and said to himself, "Everything that happens in life has a purpose. The next day the army came to town and conscripted all of the young men into the army. Of cause Jed's son had a broken leg and could not be conscripted. The towns' people said "What good luck." And you know what Jed said. I can keep going with the story although I think you now have the idea.

We don't know sometimes when something appears to go wrong whether it's leading us to the next point we need to learn, to help us achieve success. Sometimes we need to have a problem which we must overcome so we have the knowledge and skills to achieve our final objective.

A problem comes into your life and someone makes the comment "Bad luck" just answer "Good luck, or bad luck who knows." And say to yourself "Everything that happens in life has a purpose." May be it is leading to something you need to learn. Like my parking spots where I learnt.

(Important Point 2 Page 13) You can't prove this to anyone; they just have to have the faith to do it.

THE WORLD

What can we expect from this world?

What do we think is going to happen?

How do we achieve the goals we set for ourselves?

You are still connected to the Higher Self by your emotions. This world is designed to help you realise your goals.

IMPORTANT POINT 59: It is a world of emotions and we learn through emotions.

The main law on earth is THE LAW OF ATTRACTION and that means LIKE ATTRACTS LIKE.

IMPORTANT POINT 60: This means how you think is what you get.

What you think is creating your reality. The universe organises the lessons you need so you will learn in the most effective way. Everything on earth is a reflection to your knowing.

IMPORTANT POINT 61: Everything that happens around you no matter what, you have drawn to yourself.

Nothing will take place unless you need to understand, learn and grow. The universe provides it through creating the situation you need to have in your life. The question is how do you react in an emotional world?

On earth; all things are symbols to help you learn about yourself.

IMPORTANT POINT 62: Everything that comes into your life comes in for a reason.

If you look at the way you react, then you're going to learn from the situation. There are no mistakes only lessons.

IMPORTANT POINT 63: If you keep getting a problem over and over, it means you have not learnt to solve it and it probably means it's one of the lessons you came here to learn.

It's not saying you're slow it's just saying this is a lesson you need to handle a different way.

IMPORTANT POINT 64: All the time the universe is providing symbols and situations to help you learn about yourself.

You can be positive or negative. You came here to learn and understand. The answers are inside of you, because even though you do not remember, they are all available.

You are still connected to the Higher Self through your emotions. If everything is going according to plan you will feel okay, even in the midst of a difficult problem. You will feel confident and know you can handle the situation. When you feel okay, it's an indication that you are in fact on track. In that way the Higher Self manipulates you into solving your problems.

If you have any doubt, move closer to your Higher Self then you will make good decisions. If you move away from the Higher Self you will start to feel bad and you'll make bad decisions.

IMPORTANT POINT 65: The further you move away from your Higher Self you will go through upset, frustration, resentment, anger, revenge and depression.

Remember feelings are the key. If you move closer to the Higher Self you feel okay, happy, hopeful, love and then peace so that you make good decisions because you are close to what you came down to achieve.

If you get any of the feeling of upset frustration, resentment, anger, revenge or depression, realise the Higher Self is giving you a message through your emotions.

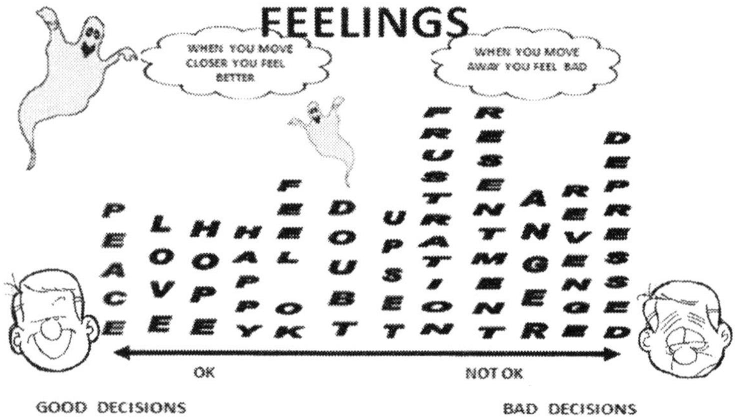

What creates emotional upsets? We are all normal people; we have likes or dislikes, as well as small phobias.

IMPORTANT POINT 66: Whatever you believe is reality, becomes reality. What you believe is truth, becomes your truth, and you will go out of your way to prove it over and over again.

Remember the example of the woman **(case 15 Page 92)** whose father was a perfect example for her to follow. Yet because her belief was that all men are liars and all men are untrustworthy, she sought out and married untrustworthy men to prove it over and over. She should have challenged her belief and said here is an example of a perfect male, my father, and then she could look and find one who was trustworthy and not a liar.

YOU COME IN WITH

What are your expectations?
What do you want out of life?

IMPORTANT POINT 67: When you are born, you come in with your past life experiences. All of the alternatives that you were given in the school in the afterlife, The Elders advice, your Guides advice, your goals and expectations and your trigger points that will take place throughout your life. These become part of your hidden memory.

At the time of conception, you received the learning of your parents through their DNA. Your observations and reactions, formed while you were within the womb. The way you observe your parents and the way your parents act towards you. You have cultural concepts imposed on you. And of course one of the things I mentioned before, you will go through the 12 stages of learning.

IMPORTANT POINT 68: Over a number of lifetimes you will go through the 12 different personality characteristics contained in the signs of the zodiac.

LOGIC

IMPORTANT POINT 69: You will also learn through experience and logical reasoning.

We live in a logical world trying to make emotional decisions.

Logic may work with physical things and ideas. It is very difficult when we add the emotions of love and fear and we are here to learn about love. Yet we continue to tell people to use logic when making emotional decisions.

Let's look at logic, how it works and how it is applied. If we look at the mind as a set of scales on which we place facts on one side and the opposing facts on the other side. We then look at the scales to see which end has the most information of benefit to us. After this we develop our beliefs.

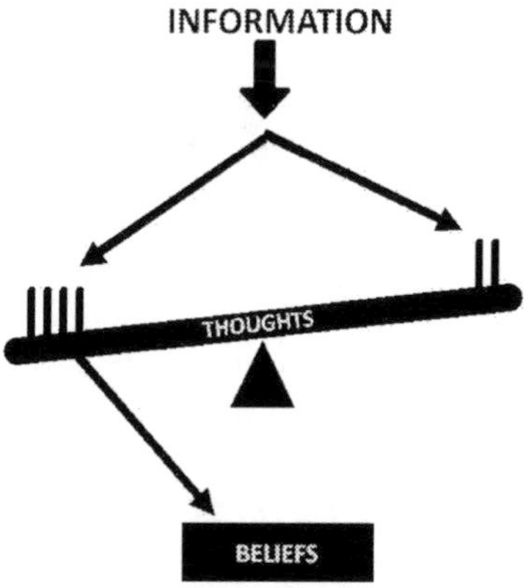

We already have facts on the scales from a previous life. In many cases this is exactly what we came to change. We add to that the culture of the country, family influences and early childhood decisions.

Logically we should keep the scales completely open to new suggestions and ideas that may cause us to change our beliefs.

We then build an attitude above the scales biased towards the weakest side. This is to protect us from getting more information which would cause us to change our mind. This too is logical because it prevents us from accepting new ideas. Otherwise we would be continually changing our mind and there would be no consistency.

Unfortunately this is illogical because we are not open to new ideas or concepts so now we are becoming more emotional.

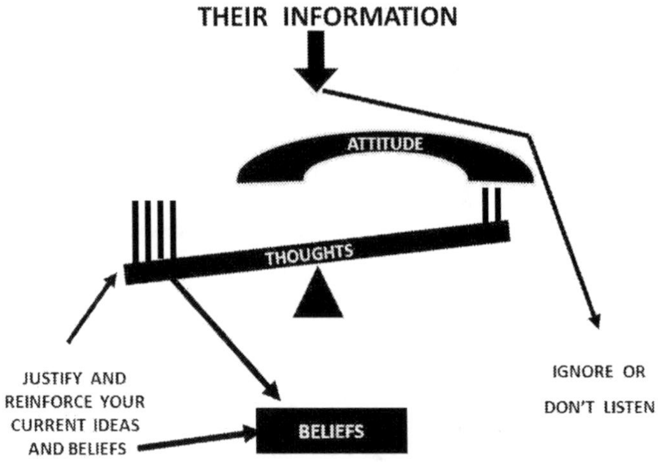

In the case of where someone has made a decision in a previous life and it has become a habit and not recognised at the conscious level, it is very difficult for them to change. **(Case 15 Page 93)** she believed all men are liars and unfaithful.

When someone is in the afterlife school, they are given alternatives. If they made a strong decision to change their beliefs, it would reinforce the subconscious and they have a better chance of the new habit working.

IMPORTANT POINT 70: On earth we need to be an open minded sceptic and move our attitude to a central passion, so information can get on both sides of the scales.

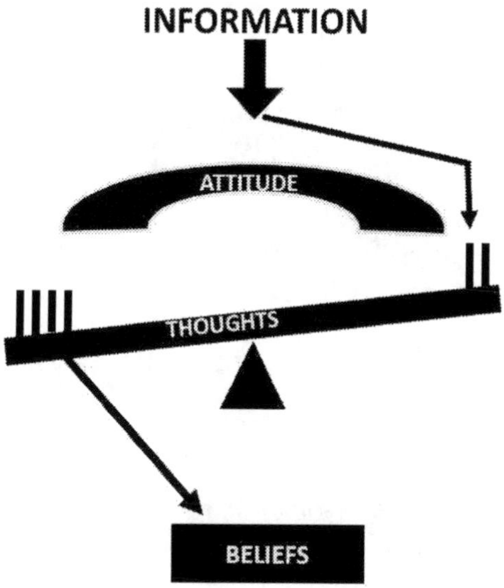

When we do this we can gather new information which may help us to overcome our fears and receive alternatives and advice which we can put on the scales. This will help us solve the problem without expecting anyone else to compensate for us and our decisions

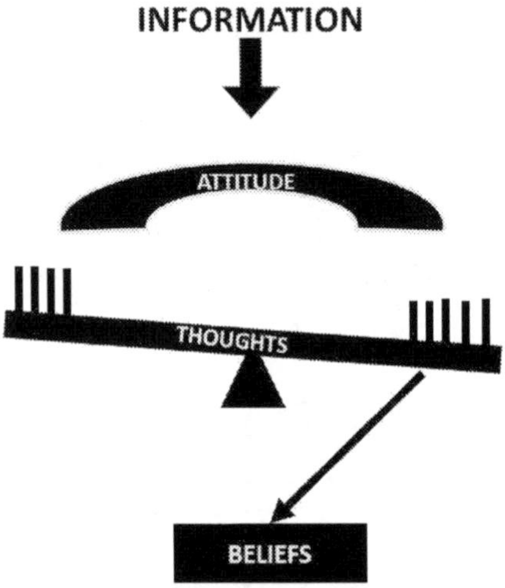

Once we have achieved new beliefs, our attitude will move again to protect our new beliefs.

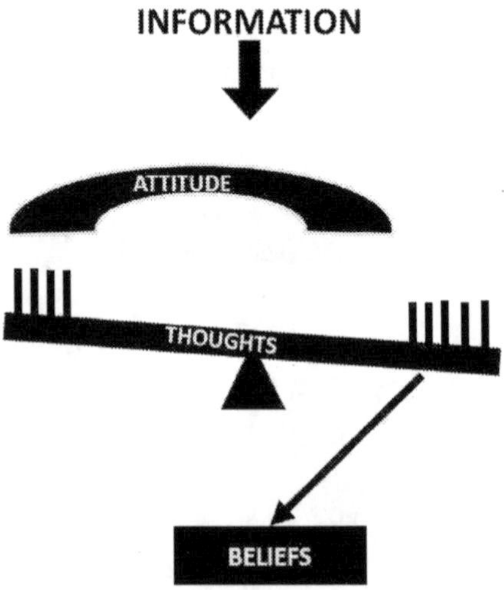

IMPORTANT POINT 71: You are only aware of 10% of your beliefs. The rest are part of your unknown belief system and they work automatically.

For example: Many men feel strange unless they sit in a particular seat in a restaurant. It is believed that they need to face the door or a window because they must keep an eye on the entrance in case danger arrives. This is believed to go back to ancient times to past lives, where men had to be prepared at all times to protect them self. We do things for a reason it is either through love or fear. A man may be fearful for his life or he may be protecting someone close to him. There can be emotional reactions from the hidden memory.

IMPORTANT POINT 72: Logic is okay for some things, yet when emotions are involved it does not seem to work.

You can make a logical decision about building a house, how many bed rooms, how many bath rooms, yet when it comes to design emotions become involved.

We often think we work something out logically. Quite often if we do not have all of the information necessary and we can make assumptions which are not true.

This brings to mind a story of a gentleman at the race track. He was deciding which horse to place a bet and in which race. He decided to stand near the starting gates and see which horse went into the barrier easily, hoping that this would indicate to him a winning horse. As the horses were put in a priest raced behind the horses, took out a small book from his pocket placed his hand on one of the horses, then he jumped over the fence and waited. The starting gates opened the horses bolted out, The race seemed to go quite quickly and the horse the priest put his hand on won. The gambler thought this is great, I must see what's going on here;

maybe it is something I need to know. The next race once again the priest raced behind the horses, took out his book read from the book placed a book back in his pocket and jumped over the fence. The race started and low and behold there was a bit of a struggle and the priest horse won. The guy thought this is amazing so he watched very carefully.

Once again the priest jumped over the fence raced behind the horses, put his hand on one of the horses, took out his little book, so the guy put everything he had on the horse to win. He got back just in time to see the horses bowled out of the starting gates. The horse the priest put his hand on seemed to be doing well then all of a sudden it stumbled and fell over and died. Well the guy could not believe this, so he went to the priest and said "What is going on the first time you put your hand on the horse it won the second time you put your hand on the horse it won and a third time the horse drops dead. The priest looked at him and said "My son my son are you a Catholic." The gambler said "What difference does that make?" And the priest said "You can't tell the difference between a blessing and the last rites."

Quite often when we think we are using logic and do not have all the facts and we can draw conclusions that are not necessarily correct.

IMPORTANT POINT 73: If you have a problem with someone in this life it needs to be solved by you. It is not someone else who creates the problem; they are only messages to you.

They are there to help you solve your situation.

IMPORTANT POINT 74: You have to change what you're thinking and change what you're doing.

You have to say "What feeling do I have? What is causing this feeling? What is the fear?" It is always an indication, that this is part of your lesson. Everything that happens in life has a purpose, everything that comes into your life you bring it to you. Two people can actually look at exactly the same situation and they will take opposite views one positive and one negative. The most important thing is what you are learning from every situation.

IMPORTANT POINT 75: It's not what happens in life it is how you view it. If you change the way you look at things, the things you look at change.

I used to have a phobia around birthdays, I seemed to go quiet and not participate fully in the celebration. At one stage Judy asked me why I went quiet. I hadn't realised it was happening. I asked my Guide to show me why I had this problem. She took me back to a time when I was eight, it was my birthday and my cousin who was one year older beat me up to show off,. This created a problem about celebrating my birthday, a hidden fear about parties, I reacted automatically. Unaware this was taking place. I guess this was something I had to learn to be myself at parties or group functions When I realized, I changed my attitude to the situation and from that time on I was okay.

IMPORTANT POINT 76: Every time you have a problem, a like or dislike, the dislike is telling you that you need to look at

the situation and see what is the fear and why you are reacting automatically.

Many people have phobias about falling off a cliff or phobias about the fear of flying, some of boats, or certain colours. Some people like timber furniture others like glass, any preferences could have come from your parents attitudes in this life or from experience in a past life. Now not all phobias create a problem they are just there because of your past experiences. Of course phobias can become dramatic and create fear. Each time you find you have negative emotions, it's a good idea to stop, sit down and ask yourself, what is it I fear in this situation?

People can get cranky for no apparent reason and become aggressive. In many cases it is automatic and is created by a fear. This fear can be hidden and could be part of their life's learning.

One guy who had a fear of falling, yet in this life he loves to fly gliders. The reason is in a past life he fell off a cliff and on the way down; he said "If I had wings I could fly." When he came into this life he overcame the fear by using gliders, to show he now has wings and can fly. Often we don't realise the universe is putting us in a position, where we can get the answers. In fact we are being put in situations and told the answers all the time so we learn.

Some people find there are certain people they like and certain people they don't like. This of course is the emotions of love or fear and quite often we do not know why we dislike the person. It can be as simple as the colour of their clothes, their height or nationality, or they knew them from a past life. There are many triggers that can come from the past and present lives which create these instant likes or dislikes.

The reason people pick their partner is because of certain characteristics. It's called THE MARBO EFECT.

IMPORTANT POINT 77: We select a partner who has the negative characteristics of our parents.

We would run a kilometre if we knew this. Yet we have no idea and we are attracted to their good points.

IMPORTANT POINT 78: In fact we chose our partner before we came to earth. The reason we chose them is they came to help us learn by bringing up the situations we need to experience for our learning.

If we have not solved all our problems with our parents, then the problems will come up with our partner.

IMPORTANT POINT 79: Yes, others may also have a problem. First solve your problem.

If you notice yourself becoming frustrated your emotions are telling you this is one of your lessons. If the problem is reoccurring and you are not coming up with a solution that is effective. You get angry or resentful or lose your cool; this does not solve the problem. You must look at the fear. Others are mirrors to you. They are there to help you solve your problem. You can now see the universe is very clever. It is reminding you, you are moving away from the Higher Self.

IMPORTANT POINT 80: Remember if you are in a situation, you drew it to yourself. This may be one of your lessons. You are drawing it to yourself to learn. Always look and say "Why did I bring this into my life?" "What is the fear?"

If you display a weakness and show insecurity, if you are unsure of yourself you will draw people to you who become dominant or aggressive. If you learn to show strength of character, they will stop or move away.

IMPORTANT POINT 81: You teach people how to treat you.

If there are two people arguing. The question is who has the problem? The answer is both because they each have a fear. If one is becoming submissive and backing down because they fear what might happen, or is becoming more aggressive as they do not want to lose. Both should stop and say to them-selves "Why am I so angry in this situation?" Maybe there is a better way to solve this situation? Anger is only a short-term solution and the problem will reoccur until the initial fear is overcome. If you are a person who loses your cool, next time it happens, sit down with the other person and discuss what it is you really want. What is the fear? And how do you overcome it?

HOW DO I ACHIEVE THE THINGS I WANT IN THIS LIFE?

If you require something, simply, start by realising all you have to do is, *ask your guide, then they arrange, and you receive.*

Therefore if you want a parking spot, as you are driving, in your mind say I need a parking spot, (and state where it will be) visualize yourself parking where you want to park. Give your guide time to organize the space. When you get the space thank your guide, although it is not necessary. It will build your confidence and get you used to talking to your guide.

Before I go on to tell you how to achieve large goals in your life I would like to ask you some questions.

IMPORTANT POINT 82: Your past life barriers and your earth learned beliefs, if they are known or hidden can affect your success.

IMPORTANT POINT 83: You can only change what you recognise and acknowledge

It is important you are aware of how your beliefs impact on your life.

Here are some statements and questions for you to consider.

What are your beliefs about statements like?

Bad luck comes in threes.

Something that comes easy is not worth having.

Only hard work gets you to success.

Do you think, you must have the bad to appreciate the good?

Do you tell people something is obvious, when you know the answer and they don't?

Are you a perfectionist? Do you expect others to live to your standards?

Do you put others down so you feel better than them?

How do you feel about people who have a lot of money?

What is the main statement you make about money?

What is your view on owning a home, a car, a boat?

Do you believe in true love or just sex?

Do you have to be in control in a relationship?

Do you believe aggression in a relationship is okay?

Does getting angry solve problems?

Must you do the right thing and what is the right thing?

If you use your talents in a positive way visualising ways to help others and advance unity and love then your guides will bring this into your life. The universe will reward you by bringing the things you want in a positive way, On the other hand if you just want sit back and take advantage of others, eventually because you are visualising using others, your guides will bring people into your life that will use you, as you put out so you receive, for what you concentrate on is what you get.

Now let's get back to the rules, the rules are simple. The same principles apply to your larger goals as to parking spots. What you visualise is what you get .

Visualisation and imagery are two of the most important mind tool you can use and are the language of your guides.

You can improve your life by achieving the things you want by learning to utilise your subconscious mind to full advantage.

Imagine you are fishing from a boat out in the ocean. The boat has a steering wheel and an automatic pilot. You set the automatic pilot so the boat heads in a northerly direction at about two to three knots. You're sitting at the back of the boat, unfortunately not catching any fish. You decide to make a change in your direction. You move to the front of the boat, take hold of steering wheel and change direction steering the boat towards the East. You have overridden the automatic pilot. If you let go the steering wheel and go back to fishing the boat will slowly turn back to the northerly direction, the automatic pilot takes over and returns the boat back to the original compass setting. You could have changed the direction of the boat without even touching the steering wheel by changing the automatic pilot the boat would then gradually adjust to its new compass heading.

Your self-image is your automatic pilot, you are programmed to behave and respond automatically and every day you do. You think and feel according to how your automatic pilot, your self-image, is programmed.

One day you decide to make a change in your direction so you get hold of the behaviour which is like grabbing the steering wheel and heading yourself in a new direction. For example becoming a non-smoker, as long as you are consciously holding onto the steering wheel you are all right, the moment you forget to exert conscious effort and let go of your behaviour you return right back to the old habits, the old characteristics of being a smoker.

If you are overweight maybe your automatic pilot is set at 10 kilos heavier than you want to be, you decide to lose weight, you steer yourself away from the old image by grabbing the steering wheel changing your diet and using other techniques, yet the moment you let go you go back to the old image overweight. This is why so many diets fail.

Now when you're holding the steering wheel, there is tremendous tension on the system, you're holding yourself away from your subconscious image. When you force change you try to override the image of yourself.

Once you learn to reset your self-image, you no longer need to try to override your self-image. I suggest you use the tools of visualisation and imagery to reset your automatic pilot, your self-image. Once you change the self-image you no longer need to grasp the steering wheel. You can use visualisation and imagery to achieve anything you want. You are able to be the person you desire, improve your family life and your working life.

The subconscious mind has no contact with the outside world, the information it processes is the information provided by the conscious mind, therefore when you visualise something the subconscious mind cannot tell the difference between that and reality. At the conscious level you know what is going on, you can tell the difference between the experience of doing something in the physical world and doing it in the mental world and the subconscious mind cannot tell the difference. Whenever you visualise something you generate within yourself the emotional response to the visualisation and it passes from the conscious into the subconscious automatically. The subconscious will act on it as if it is true.

For example one-day you are looking in the newspaper you see an advertisement for the circus, it states they have a special lion exhibit. You decide to go and see the lions. When you arrive you find at the side of the big tent a large cage with a tarpaulin over it obviously this is the cage where the lions are kept. You lift the cover, the cage is dark. You look into the back in the cage and see an old chewed bone on the floor. The cage is empty, your eyes peer into the darkness under the cover and you see the door of the cage is open. At that precise moment you feel a heavy weight on your shoulder. The image of a lion comes into the mind, you imagine the lion's paw is on your shoulder, at the same time you hear the roar of the lion and feel the hot breath on your neck. The conscious mind immediately thinks it's a real lion and sends a message to the subconscious; it reacts by increasing your heart beat, your pulse, and your blood pressure. You drop the tarpaulin expecting to see a lion, only to find it's a friend playing a joke.

In this case the subconscious mind acted to the message there was a lion. Automatically your subconscious mind acts on an imaginary experience, the same as a real experience, it can't tell the difference. It also records the feelings associated with that image. All images are stored in the subconscious mind which affects your self-image

Your self-image is your abilities and inadequacies; it is an accumulation of all the experiences you have had in your life. These experiences may be actual or imaginary. If you want to change yourself, if you want an ability, you use visualisation with emotional content to reprogram the subconscious mind, the self-image, to what you want.

It is important to remember, not just any image will change your self-image, there is a particular way visualisation and imagery must be used. If any type of imagery would change you then every time you watch television or a great sportsman, every time you admired someone else achieving something, you would be installing that image into your subconscious and therefore altering your self-image. This does not happen because you must use imagery and imagination in a very specific way.

IMPORTANT POINT 84: The type of imagery necessary to create change is referred to as experiential imagery. It is where you see yourself in the role.

Your imagery must be in the first person; you must see yourself actually carrying out the activity with feeling. You often hear people saying things like I can't see myself earning that much money. I can't see myself being a successful manager, I can't play tennis as effectively as that; they are imagining the negative situation they are imagining failure.

There are many people who believe they are incapable of achieving success. When it is thrust upon them they destroy it in a matter of months. Someone who receives a promotion and all their life have been saying I cannot see myself as a manager, may take on the position and destroy the position and themselves very quickly.

On the other hand if you see yourself as a strong capable leader, and/or a successful business person, and/or someone who has all the money they need and can handle it well, and/or a person capable of developing and maintaining a career, and/or a person capable of making effective decisions and/or you see yourself as a warm loving member of a family. Then if you visualise these characteristics within yourself using your imagination and add the emotions this will imprint on your subconscious mind.

All meaningful long-term change starts on the inside, it must start at the subconscious level, you must use experiential imagery and then go over and over it until you accept it in the subconscious, then it becomes easy for you to carry out the activity.

IMPORTANT POINT 85: The rules are

It must be first person present tense
(See yourself doing the activity as if it already is)

You must do it with emotion
(You must feel the emotions involved)

Regularly (Go over and over it until you accept it in your subconscious)

Put simply it must be:

First person
With emotion
Regularly

You have used this type of imagery all your life. Every time you carry out an activity and it is confirmed that you were a success or a failure, the image automatically transfers to the subconscious, the self-image.

I am suggesting is now you can deliberately control the development of your self-image rather than allowing it to just happen. Once you have gained control of your subconscious you have the power to develop your own characteristics and become the person you want to be.

There is a very easy way to use visualisation it is referred to as the screen of the mind. The way you use the screen of the mind is. In your mind you see a large screen in front of you with a black frame around it. On the screen you place the negative habit or image of the situation you want to change.

Analyse it, deciding exactly what is to be changed.

Next you change the black frame to white.

Next create a movie of yourself acting out the new positive action with emotion and project it on the screen.

Once you have done this you never repeat the screen with the black frame for that particular problem.

From now on whenever you review this situation you only see the image exactly the way you want it to be and a white frame around it.

Then, during the day, act out the new habit.

Before going to sleep at night congratulate yourself on a job well done.

Once you have established your goals, next visualise them in the first person, present tense, with feeling on the Screen of the mind. To assist your visualisation you may like to develop a series of affirmations to trigger the image that will add power to your new visualisation techniques.

1: *Visualise your goal.*

(It must be first person, in full detail, present tense, as if it already is.)

2: *With feeling*

(You must do it with emotion.)

3: *Regularly*

When you wake in the morning
Go through your goals.

THE NEXT PHASE: GOING TO THE AFTER LIFE

SEEK FIRST THE
KINGDOM OF GOD

AND ALL ELSE WILL BE
ADDED UNTO YOU.

THE TIME HAS COME FOR THE SOUL TO LEAVE AND GO TO THE AFTER-LIFE

In most cases, I did not investigate this to any great extent. I normally would ask the person to go to the day before they died and tell me what age they were. On most occasions this is what they did. Some occasions I would say go to the day you died in error, and they actually go to after they died and left the body. On these occasions because we were working with their guides, their guides were still with them. I would then ask them "What was the purpose of their life?" On some occasions the soul itself would answer as in the case of the young girl who was autistic, and she stated it was to have a life without love. On other occasions, their Guide would answer, and they gave more details, as in the case of the Roman soldier where he told us, he had to combine the knowledge of his Indian life, with the strength of his Roman soldier's life**. (IMPORTANT POINT 30 Page 64)**

I did not want the person to experience any trauma during a previous death experience, as they may relive the situation and cause trauma in this lifetime.

If I felt the person had a dramatic death, I would tend to tell the soul to move out of the body and become an observer, then the person did not have the emotional experience reinforced.

I will tell you one of the incidences because I think it is important to understand how statements made at the time of death can create problems or benefits in future lives.

A woman had a dramatic death. At the time of her death she asked God if she could see her children grow up. Prayers are often answered differently to what we expect. In her next life, her prayers were granted, she had the same children as in the previous life. She had a long life where she actually saw her children grow up and become successful.

Normally when a person dies they will leave the body and they will see a light or tunnel. In cases I had I did not take them through the tunnel as this was not my area of interest, although I noticed people went through three stages.

Stage one:
IMPORTANT POINT 86: They meet their Guides.

On some occasions they would see their relatives who had previously passed over. This did not seem to take long, then they went through the tunnel.

Stage two:
IMPORTANT POINT 87: Where their Guides would go through something like a counselling session discussing their current life.

The counselling session always seen to be a positive encounter at the time. If they had a traumatic experience, they sometimes go through a process of reenergising their soul and bringing it back into a more stabilised state.

Life's traumas seem to throw the energy cycle of the soul out of balance. Other times they would go to a rest area to consider what had gone on in the previous life. Sometimes they would go to other planets, which were designed for rest and rehabilitation. Even the rehabilitation program did not always remove all of the damage to their soul and this would be brought back into the next life, for example the scar on the shoulder of the Roman solder.

One particular case I remember was a young girl who had problems, when she went to cuddle her boyfriend, she felt quite strange and her arms would go cold and her hands especially cold. This did not happen with anyone else.

We went back to find out where this came from. She had a life where she betrayed someone in authority who wanted to marry her. She ran off with someone else. When she was caught, to punish her, she was to be tortured to death. Once I realise what was about to happen I took her out of her body and said "Look down and watch what was going on." I did not make her go through the death sequence. By doing this it did not reinforce what had happened. Both her arms were cut off and she died. Once we understood what had happened, she found when she cuddled her boyfriend, the strange feeling had gone and her arms and hands remained normal.

Stage three;
IMPORTANT POINT 88: They go back to their core group where they would meet up with their previous souls group.

From there they would go to school and learn answers and alternatives to problems they encounter in their previous life and prepare for their next life.

If you have read this far through the book or you are just looking at this part, I hope the words on the pages have showed you my truth. It does not mean I want you to accept it as your truth. I hope it has made you think about your life and how good it could be if you trust the universe and you open your mind to the power of love.

ROBERT

We are the physical manifestation of the universe,
we are the creators in physical form,
We are the physical expression
of all that is.

So at this point I suggest;

You leave no stone unturned in the
quest for your souls meaning.

Seek the nooks and crannies of your mind to
find that, which is, as yet, unthought

Look for the connectiveness of seemingly separate entities.
Explore your past, the present and your family
your friends for they are all clues.

Leave aside the rights and wrongs of what has gone,
it has done just that.
Retain the lessons and plant those seeds into your life.

Be happy with yourself, you are unique and of God.

IMPORTANT POINTS IN THIS BOOK

GENERAL SYMBOLS

Animals:	
Birds:	Free thinking
Dolphins:	Intelligence or wisdom
Goat	someone you know who gives silly advice.
Horses:	Strength, freedom
Sharks:	Problems with a person
Other animals:	Attitude and feelings towards that type of animal.
Beach:	The larger the waves the more they can handle or enjoy conflict The flatter the water the less they like arguments
Beach towel:	If they are sitting or standing is a barrier to the sand .Check colour
Boat:	Goal, Look at direction and check color. If going forward should you be on it moving to goal fast. Moving **to right** is something moving out of your life. **To left** is something being delayed from coming into their life your life.

Bridge:	A way to cover over problem or to avoid contact with people. Made of wood or rock? Is it in front or behind to the left or the right?
Butterfly:	Look at colour. Tend to flit from one thing to another.
Cages:	**Behind** them felt hemmed in, in the past **In front** indicates they think they have no choice and are bound by someone else's decision.
Car:	**In car driving**, Note direction, if going forward should you be in it moving to goal your fast. **Not in car** moving **to right** is something moving out of your life quickly. **To left** is something being delayed from coming into their life or your life quickly.
Cliffs:	**In font:** barriers. Feel they must lower their standards to achieve success. Or the person is an observer of life. **To left;** barrier to intuitive answers fear of the future. **To right:** barrier to logical answers wanting to forget the past.
Fences:	Perceived barriers may be able to see past. What are they made of Wood or Rock?
Flowers:	Opportunities, gifts. Have them pick them to receive gift. The color tells you the area of gift.
Grass:	Peace.
Ground:	Look at colour.

Sloping down: Will feel as if they are losing their Self-esteem.

Sloping up: Feel they are progressing in the world.

Houses: Segmented knowledge.

(The color of roof and walls can give clues to area of concern.)

(Look at first room in house to determine what area may need attention.)

Bathroom: Health.

Bedroom: Sexual relationships.

Family room: Family relationships.

Kitchen: Food, Diet.

Lounge room: Social relationships.

Mountains: In front, goals. Number of mountains indicates number of goals Snow-capped the long-term goal is a search for knowledge.

How far How long they think before they will be achieved.

How high: How big or important.

Rocky: They see problems getting there.

Ocean liner Group of people coming or moving out of your life Look at the direction to tell which.

Paths or walkways:

Is it **smooth or rough**? This indicates their journey ahead. Look at **colour.** Is it heading towards the front to left or right of the scene?

People: Can be people they like or dislike, look at the direction they are facing or going.

Pools or lake:

In front can indicate they work with people or they think their goals can only be achieved by working with others or others will help them achieve their goals. If some small pools around them may mean they work with several different groups.

River:

From left: New people coming into their life.

From right: People coming back into their life.

To left: New people being delayed from coming into their life.

To right: Current people with whom they may be losing contact.

Rocks : Current problems.
(Look at color of rocks to determine area)

Rock wall: Barrier blocking the way.
(look at the color and size of the rocks)

Sand:

Yellow: To do with thoughts and there are plenty of new thoughts coming to them.

Golden: Indicating that God is around.

White: Indication that there is knowledge for them to learn.

Putting their feet in the sand: Indicates they are trying to understand something.

	Picking up sand: Using their hands to dig in the sand shows they are trying to grasp new information.
Shells:	Small surprise's coming soon. Pick them up and expect gift.
Shops:	What are you buying in to. Look at type of shop.
Shrubs:	Protection or barriers.
Snow:	**On the ground:** Around them indicates there is plenty of knowledge available.
	On mountain top: Long term goal is knowledge.
Timber:	Old, longstanding problems.
Trains:	**In train looking out window:** Watching life go by without being involved.
	Watching train. Note direction, if going forward should you be on it moving to goal fast.
	To right: Is something moving out of your life quickly.
	To left: Is something being delayed from coming into their life your life quickly.
Trees:	**Single trees:** Knowledge, strength, protection.
	A few trees: On right can indicate the number of different areas of learning or careers.
	Trees multiple: Protection or barriers.
Water:	A symbol of people:
	Color: Of the water Green or Blue.
	Rough: They don't mind arguments.

Smooth: They like things calm.

Cool or warm: Temperature the colder the water the slower they make friends.

Water fall: Knowledge from people.

Stand under waterfall to gain knowledge.